500

cupcakes

500
cupcakes

the only cupcake compendium you'll ever need

Fergal Connolly

SELLERS
PUBLISHING

A Quintet Book

Published by Sellers Publishing, Inc.
81 West Commercial Street, Portland, Maine 04101
For ordering information:
(800) 625-3386 Toll Free
(207) 772-6814 Fax
Visit our Web site: www.rsvp.com • E-mail: rsp@rsvp.com

President and Publisher: Ronnie Sellers
Publishing Director: Robin Haywood
Managing Editor: Mary Baldwin

ISBN 13: 978-1-56906-597-6   LOC: 2005934088
ISBN 10: 1-56906-597-7
QUIN.LCUP

This book was designed and produced by
Quintet Publishing Limited
6 Blundell Street
London N7 9BH

Project Editor: Jenny Doubt
Associate Project Editor: Rebecca Warren
Editor: Marianne Canty
Art Director: Roland Codd
Photographer: Ian Garlick
Home Economist: Fergal Connolly
Publisher: Judith More
Creative Director: Richard Dewing
Managing Editor: Jane Laing

10 9 8 7 6 5 4

Manufactured in Singapore by Pica Digital Pte Ltd.
Printed in China by SNP Leefung Printers Ltd.

contents

introduction

Whether it's their individual size, their pretty frosting, or just their ability to bring back fond memories of childhood, cupcakes really do have ultimate treat-appeal. Every generation seems to love them, and even the most curmudgeonly among us will find it hard to fight off a smile when presented with a plateful of cupcakes.

Cupcakes come in many shapes and guises, but the one thing they all have in common is that they're small, individual-sized cakes baked in a muffin pan or cup-shaped molds, which are often lined with pleated foil or paper baking cups. You can make cupcakes by baking almost any cake batter in a cup-shaped mold. Classic yellow cake or pound cake mixtures are particularly popular, but gingerbread, carrot cakes, fruit cakes, yeasted cakes, and brownies can all be transformed into cupcakes. They can be frosted, decorated, glazed, dusted, or left unadorned — and whichever you choose, they're sure to be delicious.

As well as making traditional baked cupcakes, you can steam some mixtures to make dense, moist desserts, like bread pudding. You can make other cupcakes using the no-bake method, in which you spoon a mixture of melted and dry ingredients into cupcake molds and chill or leave them to set. These unbaked cupcakes are usually served unfrosted, or simply dusted with a little confectioners' sugar or unsweetened cocoa powder.

types of cupcakes

Cupcakes go by many different names. Some describe specific types of cakes, while others are more generic, but whatever name they go by, cupcakes can be found worldwide. Even in Southeast Asia you'll find little cupcakes. In the Philippines, mooncakes — rice cakes steamed in banana leaf cups — are a delicious treat.

Many great classic cupcakes can be served frosted — chocolate buttercream cupcakes (page 32) are served with a generous smear of rich chocolate frosting. Other ones, such as vanilla cupcakes (page 21) are delicious without frosting. Madeleines are classic French cupcakes that are also served plain. Baked in a shell-shaped mold, they are traditionally made with a mixture of egg yolks beaten with sugar and lemon zest, then combined with flour, hazelnut butter, and whisked egg whites. You will find a modern recipe for madeleines on page 40. Queen cakes are a traditional British cupcake made with a creamed butter mixture combination not unlike the vanilla cupcake mixture, with currants, and lemon zest added. Traditionally, Queen cakes were baked in small, fluted molds, but today they are usually baked in paper-lined or greased muffin pans.

Muffins, a huge category of cupcakes, are leavened with baking powder (and occasionally yeast) and are often baked without paper baking cups. Depending on the amount of sugar and butter in the recipe, muffins can be eaten as a sweet breakfast treat (such as our blueberry muffins on page 161), a teatime snack (try our raspberry and coffee recipe, page 163) or a savory stopgap (such as pumpkin and ginger muffins on page 306). Muffins are usually unfrosted, although they may have a topping added before baking — for example, a sprinkling of coarse sugar, a streusal topping, or a little shredded Parmesan cheese.

frosting cupcakes

Although some cupcakes are served plain, it is the frosting that makes many cupcakes. Whether it's a thick smear of cream cheese frosting or an intricately decorated cake topped with fondant decorations, it's the topping that often causes the greatest delight, not just for the sweet, luscious flavor it adds to a simple cake. Once frosted, cupcakes are best eaten right away, and if you intend to store or freeze them, don't frost them first. Whether you are a child or adult, beginner or advanced baker, once you get started on the recipes in this book, you'll realize just how fun baking and decorating cupcakes can be!

equipment

Most cupcakes and muffins are incredibly simple to make, and you'll only need a few pieces of equipment.

scales, measuring jugs, cups, & spoons
Accurate weighing scales and/or calibrated measuring cups, as well as proper measuring spoons, are essential for successful baking. If the proportions of ingredients are incorrect, the cupcake or muffin may not rise and/or set properly.

mixing bowls and spoons
You will need a medium-sized bowl and wooden spoon for mixing most cupcake batters. Smaller-sized bowls are useful for mixing small quantities. A large metal spoon is useful for folding ingredients into delicate whisked mixtures. Unless otherwise stipulated, use a medium-sized bowl for the recipes in this book.

sieves
You will need a large sieve for sifting dry ingredients such as flour and a small one for dusting icing sugar or cocoa over baked cupcakes.

muffin pans
Muffin pans are the most user-friendly pans for making standard cupcakes. The standard muffin pan has 6 or 12 cup-shaped indentations. You can line them with paper baking cups, or simply grease them before filling them with batter. The standard muffin cup is approximately 2 1/2 in. (6 cm.) in diameter. Mini and jumbo muffin pans are a great way to vary shapes and sizes of your cupcakes. Mini muffin pans have 12 or 24 cup-shaped

indentations and are 2 in. (5 cm.) in diameter, whereas jumbo muffin pans have 6 cup-shaped indentations, with each cup measuring 4 in. (10 cm.) in diameter.

other cupcake molds
You can bake cupcakes in other molded pans. Shell-shaped madeleine pans are widely available. You may also find other pans with decorative, ridged cups in a variety of sizes. Individual stainless steel molds or ceramic cups can also be used to bake cupcakes.

baking cups
Pleated paper or foil baking cups are available in many sizes, from tiny petit four cups for making mini cupcakes and muffins, to giant baking cups for extra-big breakfast treats.

timers
Perfect timing is essential for success, so always use a timer when baking. Accurate digital timers are inexpensive and well worth the investment.

wire racks
Leave most cupcakes in the pan to cool for 5 minutes before transferring them to a wire rack to cool completely. Wire racks come in a variety of shapes and sizes.

other equipment
Electric mixers can save time and are great for combining all-in-one cake mixtures. The mixer should be set on medium speed unless otherwise indicated. A sharp, serrated knife with a pointed end can help slice the tops off cupcakes or make a hollow in which to spoon filling.

ingredients

Most cupcake mixtures have four basic ingredients: fat, sugar, eggs, and flour. Other ingredients, such as chocolate, nuts, and dried fruit, are frequently added.

butter & other fats

Sweet (unsalted) butter is usually best for cupcake mixtures; it gives a wonderfully rich flavor. For creamed cupcake mixtures, use butter at room temperature; for cut-in mixtures, use cold, firm butter; and for melted mixtures, dice the butter before gently warming it. Margarine, white cooking fats, and mild-tasting vegetable oils sometimes replace butter and are a good choice for those with a dairy intolerance or allergy. Butter and cream cheese should always be softened before adding to the recipe unless otherwise stated.

sugar & other sweeteners

There are many different types of sugar, all of which add their own unique taste and texture to cupcake mixtures. Refined white sugars add sweetness, while brown sugars add flavor and color as well. Brown sugar should always be packed when being measured. The texture of the sugar will also affect the cupcake. Superfine sugar is most frequently used for cupcakes, but coarser-textured sugars such as raw sugar, and moist sugars such as brown sugar, are also used. Confectioners' sugar is generally used for dusting cupcakes and making frosting.

Light corn syrup, maple syrup, honey, and molasses can also be used in cupcakes, either in place of, or alongside, sugar. They give a distinctive taste and texture, and are a frequent addition to melted cake mixtures.

flour & flour alternatives

Most cupcake mixtures call for self-rising flour or all-purpose flour, with the addition of a leavening agent. Whole wheat flour is sometimes used, but it produces cupcakes with a heavier, denser texture. Non-wheat flours, often combined with wheat flour, may also be used. These include cornmeal, oatmeal, cornstarch, and rice flour. Ground nuts may be used in place of flour and are particularly good for gluten-free cupcakes.

eggs
Eggs enrich cupcake mixtures and help to bind ingredients together. For the best results, use eggs at room temperature. When whisking egg whites, be sure to use a clean, grease-free bowl. Eggs should always be lightly beaten before adding to the recipe unless otherwise stated.

other ingredients & flavorings
Dried fruits, nuts, and seeds are a popular addition to cupcake mixtures. Dried fruits add natural sweetness, so you may be able to use less sugar than in a plain cupcake mixture. Different dried fruits are often interchangeable in recipes.

Fresh fruit such as mashed bananas, apples, pineapples, and berries may also be folded into cupcake batters. Frozen fruit may be substituted for the recipes in this book. Thoroughly thaw and drain before adding to the recipe.

Chocolate, another popular ingredient, may be used to flavor or bind cake mixtures or to decorate baked cupcakes. For the recipes in this book, you'll need unsweetened cocoa powder, chocolate chips or chunks, and different varieties of baking chocolate in your pantry.

Vanilla-flavored pudding or pie filling may be substituted for custard.

Always assume that herbs used in the recipes are dried, unless fresh is specified.

Other ingredients and flavorings include marshmallows, spices, cheese, vanilla, coffee, citrus zest, almond extract, orange flower water and rosewater, and liqueurs.

making cupcakes

There are four main types of cupcake mixtures. The order in which ingredients are added and the way they are combined — for example, beaten or folded in — will affect the final texture of the cupcakes.

preparing the pan
When the recipe calls for the pan to be greased, you may use any fat you choose. Smear a little butter, margarine, or olive oil on a paper towel and wipe each cup thoroughly. Low-calorie sprays can also be used for this purpose. Fill any empty cups in the pan with water.

creamed mixtures
For creamed mixtures, you begin by creaming the sugar and fat together to make a light, fluffy mixture before beating in eggs. Self-rising flour (or all-purpose flour and a leavening agent such as baking powder) is then folded in, along with any other flavoring ingredients. The mixture should then be poured into baking cups and baked immediately. Moisture and heat cause tiny bubbles of carbon dioxide to be released, producing cupcakes with a light and fluffy texture.

Sometimes baking powder may be replaced with baking soda plus an acidic ingredient, such as vinegar, cider, or buttermilk. These substitutes all work effectively to help the cupcake rise while it is baking.

all-in-one mixtures
This technique is literally "all in one": Put all the ingredients in a bowl and beat them until smooth. Then fold in additional ingredients such as dried fruit and pour the batter into the pan(s) for baking.

whisked mixtures

The classic cupcake mixture is whisked. Begin by whisking eggs and sugar. Then fold in the flour and other dry ingredients. The air bubbles expand in the heat, causing the cupcake to rise and giving it a spongy texture.

muffin mixtures

For muffins, combine the dry ingredients in one bowl, and the melted fat and any liquid ingredients in another. Pour the liquid ingredients into the dry ingredients and stir until just combined. Overmixing will give tough, chewy results, rather than light, fluffy muffins — so don't worry if there are still a few streaks of flour in the batter as you spoon it into the cups.

general baking tips

When adding batter to a pan, you may either spoon or pour the batter into the cups. Each cup should be two-thirds full unless otherwise stated. When baking, the pans should be placed in the center of the oven. As oven temperatures vary by model, test cupcakes for doneness a few minutes before the end of the baking time. If a skewer inserted into the center of the cupcake comes out clean, it is done. If your cupcakes are brown on top but not cooked through, try lowering your oven temperature.

storing

Cupcakes made with a high proportion of fat can be stored in an airtight container for several days. Muffins and low-fat cupcakes are usually best eaten on the day of making. For the best results, store cakes unfrosted, and frost on the day of serving. Cupcakes can also be frozen, unfrosted, in an airtight container for up to 3 months.

decorating cupcakes

Golden muffins look fabulous unfrosted — risen and craggy with their puffed-up tops — but cupcakes are the treats that you can really go to town on when it comes to decoration. A simple spoonful of frosting with a cherry on top or a drizzle of melted chocolate is just the start. Supermarkets and specialty cooking stores sell a host of ingredients and equipment to help you — from food coloring and ready-made frostings to edible sugared flowers and brightly colored candy. Here are a few ideas that will help you transform the simplest cupcakes into a stunning dessert.

getting started
If you're going for simply frosted cupcakes — perhaps with a dollop of frosting and a big colored candy or whole nut on top — leave the cupcake as it is, with its domed top. However, if you want to go for a more intricately decorated cupcake — perhaps with a patterned frosting on top, or lots of candies — slice off the top of the cake to give you a flat surface. Always wait for cupcakes to cool before frosting them.

decorating cupcakes before baking
Unbaked cupcakes and muffins can be sprinkled with coarse sugar; whole, chopped, or flaked nuts or dried fruit; or a piece of fresh fruit such as a slice of apple or peach. Don't top them with anything too heavy or it may sink into the batter during baking. Finely shredded Parmesan cheese can make a good topping for savory muffins.

dusting and sprinkling
The simplest way to decorate freshly baked cupcakes is to dust them with confectioners' sugar or unsweetened cocoa.

fondant frosting

Perfect for rolling out and draping over cupcakes, this firm frosting can also be colored and made into shapes to decorate cakes. You can make it yourself, but it's much easier to buy ready-to-roll fondant frosting and color it yourself. Simply add a few drops of food coloring and then thoroughly knead the fondant. Repeat until the desired color is achieved.

colored candy & cake decorations

Candy and colored sprinkles are easy ways to decorate cupcakes. Alternately, look in specialty cooking stores for sugar flowers, pastel-colored almonds, and other edible decorations. First top the cupcakes with frosting or melted chocolate, then allow it to set slightly before pressing on the decorations. If you prefer a cupcake without too much frosting, use only a small blob to attach individual candies or decorations — they'll look just as good but won't be nearly so sweet.

fresh fruit

Summer berries look delightful (and taste delectable) on top of frosted cupcakes. They're particularly good on cakes topped with buttercream or cream cheese frosting. Or even simpler, just spoon a big dollop of heavy cream on top of each cupcake and top with a few fresh raspberries or strawberries.

simple fillings

The simplest filling is flavored heavy cream. Try sweetening heavy cream with a little confectioners' sugar and adding a few drops of vanilla or peppermint extract, rosewater, or citrus zest. Honey and maple syrup make good flavorings, as do liqueurs such as Cointreau.

serving ideas & cupcake gifts

Cupcakes are often associated with children, but offer a plate of cupcakes to grown adults and you're sure to see their faces light up. Whether it's a rack of warm, wholesome muffins or a glittering cake stand piled high with pretty, pastel-colored confections, cupcakes are always a hit and seem to appeal to every generation.

cakes on the move

Baked in their own wrappers, these lovely cakes aren't just for eating at home. An individual, portion-sized cake is great for eating on the move — whether it's a breakfast muffin to eat on the run, a treat to go in a lunchbox, an energy-boosting snack to take on a long walk, or an easy dessert to serve at a picnic.

dashing desserts

There's something wonderfully informal yet utterly appealing about cupcakes that makes them a great alternative to dessert after a special meal. Who's got time to make a dessert after an appetizer and main course — and who's really got room to fit one in? Why not bring out a plate of sophisticated cupcakes with coffee instead? You're sure to get just as much praise as you would for a dessert that takes hours to make.

celebrating with cupcakes

Big celebration cakes are a thing of the past. What everyone wants now is a towering pile of cupcakes. For birthdays, pile up cupcakes on a plate and stick them with birthday candles and baby indoor sparklers to really get the celebrations going. This alternative to the traditional cake is particularly good for kids' parties, where little children can struggle with a big slice of cake — or for adult parties where everyone is trying to watch their waistline!

Huge tiered wedding cakes are off the agenda for those in the know. For a real impact at your wedding, go for pretty white wedding cupcakes piled high on a cake stand or arranged in tiers. It makes serving so much easier — and guests will love them.

Spoil your loved one with love-heart cupcakes (page 208) on Valentine's Day, or scare them at Halloween with a plate of Halloween pumpkin muffins (page 198). Show your patriotic pride with a tray of Independence Day cupcakes (page 207), and on St. Patrick's Day, start the celebrations at breakfast time with a special St. Patrick's Day muffin (page 193).

special gifts

Cupcakes make great gifts, and you're sure to put a smile on the face of the recipient. They're usually best packed in a single layer, with a little tissue paper tucked around them to make sure they don't shift as you transport them. Pretty boxes with clear plastic lids are a good choice, particularly for cupcakes with decorative frosting. They're available from stationery and department stores, so look around and see what you can find.

Flat baskets make another pretty way to deliver your cupcakes. Arrive at a brunch party with a basket full of warm muffins and your host — and the other guests — will love you for them!

Cupcakes with a firm frosting (such as fondant or royal frosting) can look pretty wrapped up individually in clear cellophane. Cut out a large square of cellophane, place a cupcake in the center, then pull up the edges around the cake and tie with ribbon. These individually wrapped cakes make great going-home presents after a kids' party or festive wedding favors.

You can also decorate the foil or paper baking cups that contain the cupcakes. Try tying ribbon around each baking cup, or cut out a round of pretty fabric, place the cupcake in the center, and tie up firmly with coordinating ribbon.

classic cupcakes

These cupcakes have delighted generations. From the classic
combination of apple and cinnamon to the irresistibly rich pairing
of rum and raisin, all the best-loved recipes are here.

spanish orange syrup cupcakes

see variations page 42

Make these sticky cupcakes ahead of time to let the syrup soak through.

for the cupcakes
2 medium, seedless sweet oranges,
    peeled and roughly chopped
1/2 cup (1 stick) sweet butter
1 cup superfine sugar
2 eggs
1/2 cup semolina

1/2 cup almond meal
1/2 cup self-rising flour

for the syrup
1 peeled orange rind, from cupcake recipe
1/2 cup superfine sugar
1 cup water

Preheat the oven to 325°F (160°C). Place 12 paper baking cups in a muffin pan. In a saucepan, cover the oranges with water. Simmer until tender, about 15 minutes. Cool. Drain the oranges and purée in a food processor. In a bowl, beat the butter and sugar with an electric mixer until light. Slowly beat in the eggs. Stir in the rest of the ingredients, along with the orange purée, until well combined. Spoon the mixture into the cups. Bake for 35 minutes. Remove pan from the oven and cool.

To make the syrup, thinly slice the orange rind, removing the pith. Cut the orange rind into thin strips. In a pan, bring the sugar and water to a simmer, stirring to dissolve the sugar. Add the orange strips and boil uncovered for 5 minutes, or until tender. Spoon the syrup onto each cupcake. Store in an airtight container for up to 2 days.

Makes 1 dozen

vanilla cupcakes

see variations page 43

The grand dame of cupcakes. If you can get vanilla sugar, use half regular superfine and half vanilla superfine. This will really enhance the vanilla flavor.

1 cup (2 sticks) sweet butter, softened
1 cup superfine sugar
2 cups self-rising flour

1 tsp. baking powder
4 eggs
1 tsp. vanilla extract

Preheat the oven to 350°F (175°C). Place 18 paper baking cups in muffin pans.

Place all the ingredients in a medium bowl and beat with an electric mixer until smooth and pale, about 2 to 3 minutes.

Spoon the mixture into the cups. Bake for 20 minutes.

Remove the pans from the oven and cool for 5 minutes. Then remove the cupcakes and cool on a rack.

Store in an airtight container for up to 3 days, or freeze for up to 3 months.

Makes 1 1/2 dozen

gingerbread pots

see variations page 44

You could make these dense, sticky gingerbread cupcakes in terra cotta pots to give them a rustic charm. The sharp lemon drizzle helps to cut the sweetness of the gingerbread.

for the gingerbread
1 cup self-rising flour
1 cup whole wheat self-rising flour
1 tbsp. baking powder
4 tsp. ground ginger
1 tsp. cinnamon
1 cup packed unrefined brown sugar
2 eggs

1/2 cup honey
1/2 cup butter, melted
3/4 cup milk
2 tbsp. roughly chopped candied ginger

for the drizzle
1 cup confectioners' sugar
5 tbsp. lemon juice

Preheat the oven to 350°F (175°C). Place 12 paper baking cups in a muffin pan or line 12 small terra cotta pots with baking parchment. Sift the flours, baking powder, ginger, and cinnamon into a large bowl. In a medium bowl combine the remaining ingredients and beat with an electric mixer until smooth, about 2 to 3 minutes. Stir into the dry ingredients. Spoon the batter into the cups.

Bake for 20 minutes. Remove pan or pots from the oven and cool for 10 minutes. Then remove cupcakes and cool on a rack. To make the drizzle, sift the confectioners' sugar into a bowl and slowly add the lemon juice, stirring until just combined. Drizzle over the tops of the cupcakes. Store in an airtight container for up to 3 days.

Makes 1 dozen

lemon butterfly cupcakes

see variations page 45

You'll love these delicate little numbers, which can be served with tea or as a dessert.

for the cupcakes
1 cup (2 sticks) sweet butter, softened
1 cup superfine sugar
2 cups self-rising flour
1 tsp. baking powder
4 eggs
1 tsp. vanilla extract

for the frosting
1/2 cup (1 stick) sweet butter
2 cups confectioners' sugar, sifted
1 tsp. vanilla extract
1 tbsp. lemon zest

Preheat the oven to 350°F (175°C). Place 18 paper baking cups in muffin pans. Combine all ingredients for the cupcakes in a large bowl and beat with an electric mixer until smooth and pale, about 2 to 3 minutes. Spoon the batter into the cups.

Bake for 20 minutes. Remove pans from the oven and cool for 5 minutes. Then remove the cupcakes and cool on a rack. Prepare the frosting by beating the butter, confectioners' sugar, vanilla, and lemon zest until smooth. Cut a slice from the top of each cake and cut it into two. Pipe the frosting onto the flattened top of each cupcake. Then place the half-circles of cake at an angle on each side of the frosting.

Store unfrosted in an airtight container for up to 3 days, or freeze for up to 3 months.

Makes 1 1/2 dozen

rum & raisin cupcakes

see variations page 46

Use dark rum in this recipe to give these cupcakes a warm Caribbean feel.

for the cupcakes
1/2 cup (3 1/2 oz.) raisins
3 tbsp. dark rum
1 cup (2 sticks) sweet butter, softened
1 cup superfine sugar
2 cups self-rising flour

1 tsp. baking powder
4 eggs

for the syrup
5 tbsp. dark rum
2 tbsp. unpacked light brown sugar

Soak the raisins in the rum for 2 to 3 hours or overnight to soften them. Drain. Preheat the oven to 350°F (175°C). Place 18 paper baking cups in muffin pans. Combine all the cupcake ingredients in a large bowl and beat with an electric mixer until smooth and pale, about 2 to 3 minutes. Stir in the raisins. Spoon the batter into the cups. Bake for 20 minutes.

While the cupcakes are in the oven, combine the syrup ingredients in a pan. Over low heat, dissolve the sugar in the rum. Simmer for 5 minutes, then remove from the heat. Remove pans from the oven. With a toothpick, prick 5 holes in each cupcake and pour the warm syrup over them. Then remove the cupcakes and cool on a rack.

Store in an airtight container for up to 3 days, or freeze for up to 3 months.

Makes 1 1/2 dozen

mini raspberry & coconut cupcakes

see variations page 47

The inspiration for these cupcakes came from the classic English Bakewell tart.

3 tbsp. almond meal
1/2 cup (2 1/2 oz.) flaked coconut
1 1/2 cups confectioners' sugar, sifted
1 1/2 cups all-purpose flour
1 tsp. baking powder

1/2 cup (1 stick) sweet butter, melted
5 egg whites
1 cup fresh or thawed, frozen raspberries
2 tbsp. shredded coconut

Preheat the oven to 375°F (190°C). Place 24 mini ceramic baking cups on a cookie sheet.

In a large bowl, combine the almond meal, coconut, confectioners' sugar, flour, and baking powder. Stir in the butter, followed by the egg whites.

Spoon the mixture into the cups. Drop a raspberry and some of the shredded coconut on top of each cupcake. Bake for 12 to 15 minutes. Remove the cups from the oven and cool for 5 minutes. Then remove the cupcakes and cool on a rack.

Store in an airtight container for up to 2 days, or freeze in sealed containers for up to 3 months.

Makes 2 dozen

carrot & walnut cupcakes

see variations page 48

Carrot cake somehow doesn't seem to be as naughty as other cakes!

for the cupcakes
1 cup (2 sticks) sweet butter, softened
1 cup superfine sugar
2 cups self-rising flour
4 eggs
1 tsp. allspice
1 cup (3 1/2 oz.) chopped walnuts
1 cup freshly shredded carrots
2 tbsp. golden raisins

for the frosting
1 cup cream cheese, softened
1 1/2 cups confectioners' sugar, sifted
1 tbsp. lemon juice
1 tsp. vanilla extract
3 tbsp. chopped walnuts

Preheat the oven to 350°F (175°C). Place 18 baking cups in muffin pans. Combine the butter, sugar, flour, and eggs in a large bowl and beat with an electric mixer until smooth, about 2 to 3 minutes. Stir in the rest of the ingredients. Spoon the batter into the cups. Bake for 20 minutes. Remove pans from the oven and cool for 5 minutes. Then remove the cupcakes and cool on a rack. To make the frosting, slowly beat the cream cheese and confectioners' sugar in a large bowl with an electric mixer until creamy and soft. Add the lemon juice and vanilla and beat briskly until well combined. Spread the frosting liberally onto the cooled cupcakes and garnish with the chopped walnuts.

Store unfrosted for up to 3 days in an airtight container, or freeze for up to 3 months.

Makes about 1 1/2 dozen

very cherry cupcakes

see variations page 49

Maraschino cherries give these cupcakes a wonderful rich flavor.

for the cupcakes
1 cup (2 sticks) sweet butter, softened
1 cup superfine sugar
2 cups self-rising flour
1 tsp. baking powder
4 eggs
2 tbsp. kirsch

for the frosting
3 cups confectioners' sugar, sifted
1 cup (2 sticks) sweet butter
Pinch of salt
Red food coloring
12 bottled morello or maraschino cherries
    with stems

Preheat the oven to 350°F (175°C). Place 18 paper baking cups in muffin pans.

Combine all the cupcake ingredients in a large bowl and beat with an electric mixer until smooth, about 2 to 3 minutes. Spoon the batter into the cups. Bake for 20 minutes. Remove pans from the oven and cool for 5 minutes. Then remove the cupcakes and cool on a rack. To make the frosting, beat the confectioners' sugar, butter, and salt in a medium bowl with an electric mixer until smooth. Add a few drops of the food coloring and beat until well combined and pink. Spread the frosting onto the cooled cupcakes and garnish with a cherry.

Store unfrosted in an airtight container for up to 3 days, or freeze for up to 3 months.

Makes 1 1/2 dozen

classic chocolate buttercream cupcakes

see variations page 50

The semisweet chocolate in this recipe gives the frosting a wonderful glossy sheen.

for the cupcakes
1 cup (2 sticks) sweet butter, softened
1 cup superfine sugar
1 1/2 cups self-rising flour
1 tsp. baking powder
4 tbsp. Dutch-process cocoa powder
4 eggs
1 tsp. vanilla extract

for the frosting
1 1/2 cups (10 1/2 oz.) chopped semisweet
    chocolate
2 tbsp. heavy cream
1/2 cup (1 stick) sweet butter, softened
1 1/2 cups confectioners' sugar, sifted

Preheat the oven to 350°F (175°C). Place 18 paper baking cups in muffin pans. Combine all the cupcake ingredients in a large bowl and beat with an electric mixer until smooth, about 2 to 3 minutes. Spoon the batter into the cups. Bake for 20 minutes. Remove pans from the oven and cool for 5 minutes. Then remove the cupcakes and cool on a rack. For the frosting, put the chocolate, cream, and butter in a pan over low heat. Stir gently until combined. Remove from the heat and stir in the confectioners' sugar until the mixture is smooth. Swirl onto the cupcakes.

Store unfrosted in an airtight container for up to 2 days.

Makes 1 1/2 dozen

applesauce &
cinnamon cupcakes

see variations page 51

Cinnamon brings a delicate sweetness to this cupcake recipe and complements the applesauce marvelously.

1/2 cup (1 stick) sweet butter, softened
1/2 cup plus 1 tbsp. superfine sugar
1 cup self-rising flour
2 eggs
3/4 cup unsweetened applesauce
3/4 tsp. cinnamon

1/2 cup (3 1/2 oz.) chopped pecans
1/2 cup (3 1/2 oz.) golden raisins
1 small red eating apple, thinly sliced
2 tbsp. granulated sugar

Preheat the oven to 350°F (175°C). Grease a 12-cup muffin pan. Place the butter, sugar, flour, and egg in a bowl and beat with an electric mixer until smooth and pale, about 2 to 3 minutes. Stir in the applesauce, cinnamon, pecans, and raisins.

Spoon the batter into the cups. Lay the apple slices on top and sprinkle with a little sugar.

Bake for 25 minutes. Remove pan from the oven and cool for 5 minutes. Then remove the cupcakes and cool on a rack. Serve warm.

Store in an airtight container for up to 3 days, or freeze for up to 3 months.

Makes 1 dozen

peanut butter cupcakes

see variations page 52

The texture of crunchy peanut butter in this recipe is excellent, though creamier varieties also work.

for the cupcakes
1 cup (2 sticks) sweet butter, softened
1 cup superfine sugar
2 cups self-rising flour
4 eggs
1 cup crunchy peanut butter

for the frosting
1/2 cup crunchy peanut butter
1/2 cup (1 stick) sweet butter, softened
2 tsp. vanilla extract
2 cups confectioners' sugar, sifted
2 tbsp. milk

Preheat the oven to 350°F (175°C). Place 18 paper baking cups in muffin pans. Combine the butter, sugar, flour, and eggs in a large bowl and beat with an electric mixer until smooth, about 2 to 3 minutes. Stir in the peanut butter until well combined. Spoon the batter into the cups. Bake for 20 minutes. Remove pans from the oven and cool for 5 minutes. Then remove the cupcakes and cool on a rack.

To make the frosting, combine the peanut butter, butter, and vanilla in a medium bowl. Using an electric mixer beat until light and fluffy, about 1 to 2 minutes. Add the confectioners' sugar along with the milk, and beat until well combined. Swirl the frosting onto the cooled cupcakes.

Store unfrosted in an airtight container for up to 3 days, or freeze for up to 3 months.

Makes 1 1/2 dozen

poppy seed cupcakes with lemon drizzle

see variations page 53

The poppy seeds give these cupcakes a wonderful crunch!

for the cupcakes
1 cup (2 sticks) sweet butter, softened
1 cup superfine sugar
2 cups self-rising flour
4 eggs
1 tsp. vanilla extract
1 tbsp. poppy seeds
1 tbsp. grated lemon zest

for the drizzle
1 cup confectioners' sugar
4 tbsp. lemon juice
2 tbsp. poppy seeds

Preheat the oven to 350°F (175°C). Place 18 paper baking cups in muffin pans. Combine the butter, sugar, flour, and eggs in a large bowl and beat with an electric mixer until smooth, about 2 to 3 minutes. Stir in the vanilla, poppy seeds, and lemon zest until well combined. Spoon the batter into the cups. Bake for 20 minutes. Remove pans from the oven and cool for 5 minutes. Then remove the cupcakes and cool on a rack. To make the drizzle, sift the confectioners' sugar into a bowl and stir in the lemon juice until it resembles the consistency of heavy cream. Stir in the poppy seeds and drizzle over the cupcakes.

Store in an airtight container for up to 2 days, or freeze for up to 3 months.

Makes 1 1/2 dozen

banana cupcakes

see variations page 54

The subtle flavor of banana perfectly complements the cream cheese frosting.

for the cupcakes
1 cup (2 sticks) sweet butter, softened
1 cup superfine sugar
2 cups self-rising flour
4 eggs
1/4 tsp. nutmeg
1 cup (about 2 large) mashed ripe bananas

for the frosting
1 cup cream cheese
1 1/2 cups confectioners' sugar, sifted
1 tbsp. lemon juice
1 tsp. vanilla extract
1 banana, thinly sliced

Preheat the oven to 350°F (175°C). Place 18 paper baking cups in muffin pans. Combine the butter, sugar, flour, eggs, and nutmeg in a large bowl and beat with an electric mixer until smooth, about 2 to 3 minutes. Stir in the mashed bananas until well combined. Spoon the batter into the cups. Bake for 20 minutes. Remove pans from the oven and cool for 5 minutes. Then remove the cupcakes and cool on a rack.

To make the frosting, slowly beat the cream cheese in a large bowl with an electric mixer until it is soft and smooth. Add the confectioners' sugar, lemon juice, and vanilla. Beat briskly until smooth and well combined. Swirl the frosting onto the cooled cupcakes. Decorate each cupcake with a banana slice.

Store unfrosted in an airtight container for up to 3 days, or freeze for up to 3 months.

Makes 1 1/2 dozen

madeleines

see variations page 55

These light, shell-shaped cupcakes hail from the town of Commercy in the Lorraine region of France.

for the madeleines
4 eggs
1 cup superfine sugar
1 cup all-purpose flour
1 tsp. baking powder
1/2 cup (1 stick) sweet butter, melted
   and cooled
1 tbsp. grated lemon zest

for the glaze
3 cups confectioners' sugar, sifted
1 cup (2 sticks) sweet butter, softened
Pinch of salt
1 tbsp. grated orange zest
Confectioners' sugar, for dusting

Preheat the oven to 350°F (175°C). Grease a pan for 18 small madeleines. In a medium bowl, beat the eggs and sugar until pale and thick. Sift the flour and baking powder into a separate medium bowl. Slowly add the flour to the egg mixture. Pour in the melted butter and stir in the lemon zest. Refrigerate for 20 minutes. Spoon the batter into the pan, filling each mold about two-thirds full. Bake for 20 minutes. Remove pan from the oven and cool for 10 minutes. Then remove the madeleines and cool on a rack. To make the glaze, beat the confectioners' sugar, butter, salt, and orange zest in a bowl using an electric mixer until smooth. Smear a little glaze on each madeleine and dust with confectioners' sugar.

Store in an airtight container up to 2 days, or freeze for up to 3 months.

Makes 1 1/2 dozen

variations

spanish orange syrup cupcakes

see base recipe page 19

blood orange syrup cupcakes
Prepare the basic cupcake recipe, substituting blood oranges for the sweet oranges.

orange & lemon syrup cupcakes
Prepare the basic cupcake recipe, adding 2 tablespoons lemon juice to the orange purée. For the syrup, zest 1 medium lemon and add with the orange zest to the water and sugar syrup.

grapefruit & orange syrup cupcakes
Prepare the basic cupcake recipe. Add 2 tablespoons grapefruit juice to the orange purée. For the syrup, zest half a medium grapefruit and add it with the orange zest to the water and sugar syrup.

variations

vanilla cupcakes

see base recipe page 21

saffron cupcakes
Prepare the basic cupcake recipe. Add a pinch of saffron to 2 tablespoons
boiling water. Infuse for 5 minutes. After creaming the cupcake ingredients,
stir in saffron and water.

almond cupcakes
Prepare the basic cupcake recipe, adding 3 tablespoons ground almond
to the mixture and substituting 1 teaspoon almond extract for the
vanilla extract.

vanilla & raisin cupcakes
Prepare the basic cupcake recipe. After creaming the cupcake ingredients,
stir in 1/2 cup (3 1/2 oz.) golden raisins.

variations

gingerbread pots

see base recipe page 22

fruity pots
Fold 1/2 cup (3 1/2 oz.) mixed chopped dried apricots, raisins, and
golden raisins to the egg mixture before stirring into the dry ingredients.

rhubarb pots
Add 1/2 cup (3 1/2 oz.) cooked sweetened rhubarb to the egg mixture
before stirring in the dry ingredients.

banana pots
Add one mashed banana to the egg mixture before stirring in the
dry ingredients.

variations

lemon butterfly cupcakes

see base recipe page 25

orange & lemon butterfly cupcakes
Prepare the basic cupcake recipe. Add 1 1/2 tablespoons grated orange zest to the frosting mixture.

red currant butterfly cupcakes
Prepare the basic cupcake recipe. Lightly crush 1/3 cup fresh or thawed frozen red currants with a fork and add to the frosting mixture.

hazelnut & raisin butterfly cupcakes
Prepare the basic cupcake recipe. Stir 3 tablespoons roughly chopped toasted hazelnuts and 2 tablespoons golden raisins into the creamed frosting mixture.

variations

rum & raisin cupcakes

see base recipe page 26

orange liqueur & candied peel cupcakes
Prepare the basic cupcake recipe, substituting orange liqueur for the rum and 1/2 cup (3 1/2 oz.) chopped candied peel for the raisins.

vodka, chili, & chocolate chip cupcakes
Prepare the basic cupcake recipe. Substitute vodka for the rum. Add 1 tablespoon seeded and finely chopped chilies and 1/2 cup (3 1/2 oz.) semisweet chocolate chips in place of the raisins.

malibu & pineapple cupcakes
Prepare the basic cupcake recipe, substituting Malibu for the rum and 1/2 cup (3 1/2 oz.) finely chopped dried pineapple for the raisins.

mini raspberry & coconut cupcakes

see base recipe page 29

mini blueberry & coconut cupcakes
Prepare the basic cupcake recipe, substituting blueberries for the raspberries.
Add 1 tablespoon finely grated lime zest.

mini blackberry & coconut cupcakes
Prepare the basic cupcake recipe, substituting 1/2 cup blackberries for the
raspberries.

mini lime, mango, & coconut cupcakes
Prepare the basic cupcake recipe, substituting 1/2 cup finely chopped fresh
or frozen mango and 1 tablespoon finely grated lime zest for the raspberries.

variations

carrot & walnut cupcakes

see base recipe page 30

coffee & walnut-frosted carrot cupcakes
Prepare the basic cupcake recipe. Add 1 teaspoon hot coffee, 1 teaspoon instant coffee granules, and 1 teaspoon coffee liqueur to the frosting mixture. Swirl the coffee frosting on top of the cupcakes, and garnish with chopped walnuts.

orange cream cheese-frosted carrot cupcakes
Prepare the basic cupcake recipe. To make the frosting, substitute 1 tablespoon orange juice for the lemon juice. Swirl the frosting and garnish with chopped walnuts and finely grated lemon zest.

mascarpone-frosted carrot cupcakes
Prepare the basic cupcake recipe. To make the frosting, substitute 1 cup (8 oz.) mascarpone for the cream cheese.

variations

very cherry cupcakes

see base recipe page 31

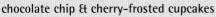

chocolate chip & cherry-frosted cupcakes
Prepare the basic cupcake recipe. Stir 1/2 cup (3 1/2 oz.) semisweet
chocolate chips into the frosting mixture after adding the food coloring.

almond & cherry-frosted cupcakes
Prepare the basic cupcake recipe, adding 3 tablespoons ground almond to
the batter mixture. Sprinkle 2 tablespoons of toasted almonds on top of the
frosting, and garnish each with a cherry.

crispy meringue & cherry-frosted cupcakes
Prepare the basic cupcake recipe. Place 4 small meringue shells in a plastic
food storage bag and lightly crush them with a rolling pin. Gently stir into
the frosting mixture after adding the food coloring. Swirl onto the cupcakes.

variations

classic chocolate buttercream cupcakes

see base recipe page 32

white & semisweet choc buttercream cupcakes
Prepare the basic cupcake recipe, stirring 3 tablespoons mixed semisweet
chocolate chips and white chocolate chips into the creamed batter.

macadamia nut-frosted buttercream cupcakes
Prepare the basic cupcake recipe. Lightly toast 1/2 cup (3 1/2 oz.) macadamia
nuts and chop finely. Stir the macadamia nuts into the frosting mixture after
adding the sugar.

orange & semisweet choc buttercream cupcakes
Prepare the basic cupcake recipe, substituting 1 tablespoon orange zest for
the vanilla extract.

applesauce & cinnamon cupcakes

see base recipe page 35

applesauce & pear cupcakes

Prepare the basic cupcake recipe. Substitute 1 ripe and firm, medium pear for the apple. Lay slices on top of each cupcake and sprinkle with sugar.

applesauce & warm caramel cupcakes

Prepare the basic cupcake recipe. To make a caramel topping, place 2 cups (6 oz.) caramels in a medium pan with 3 tablespoons evaporated milk. Heat gently, stirring until all the caramels have melted. Prick the top of the cupcakes with a toothpick and spoon the melted caramel over the cooled cakes. Then lay slices of apple on top of each cupcake.

applesauce & brandy drizzle cupcakes

Prepare the basic cupcake recipe. To make the drizzle, combine 4 tablespoons apple brandy with 3 tablespoons sugar in a medium pan. Simmer gently for 5 minutes, then spoon over the cupcakes. Then lay slices of apple on top of each cupcake.

variations

peanut butter cupcakes

see base recipe page 36

peanut butter & jam cupcakes

Prepare the basic cupcake recipe. When the cupcakes have cooled, use a sharp knife to slice off the tops. Using a teaspoon, hollow out a small hole in the top of each cupcake. Spoon 1/2 teaspoon strawberry or raspberry jam into the small hole. Place the top back on the cupcake and frost.

chocolate peanut butter cupcakes

Prepare the basic cupcake recipe. Add 1/2 cup (3 1/2 oz.) semisweet chocolate chips to the batter.

peanut butter cupcakes with fudge-frosting

Prepare the basic cupcake recipe. For the frosting, substitute smooth peanut butter for the crunchy. Add 2 tablespoons Dutch-process cocoa powder to the frosting mixture after adding the milk.

variations

poppy seed cupcakes with lemon drizzle

see base recipe page 37

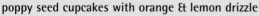

poppy seed cupcakes with orange & lemon drizzle
Prepare the basic cupcake recipe using 1/2 tablespoon orange zest and
1/2 tablespoon lemon zest. To make the drizzle, use only 2 tablespoons
lemon juice and 2 tablespoons orange juice.

poppy seed & blueberry cupcakes with lime drizzle
Prepare the basic cupcake recipe. After creaming the batter, stir in 1/2 cup
blueberries, and substitute 1 tablespoon finely grated lime zest for the
lemon zest.

poppy seed & cranberry cupcakes with lemon drizzle
Prepare the basic cupcake recipe. After creaming the batter, stir 1/2 cup
(3 1/2 oz.) dried chopped cranberries.

variations

banana cupcakes

see base recipe page 39

chocolate chip & banana cupcakes
Prepare the basic cupcake recipe. Stir in 1/2 cup (3 1/2 oz.) semisweet
chocolate chips along with the mashed bananas.

cinnamon & oat-topped banana cupcakes
Prepare the basic cupcake recipe. Place 3 tablespoons granulated sugar,
1 teaspoon cinnamon, 2 tablespoons softened sweet butter, 4 tablespoons
rolled oats, and 1 tablespoon flour in a medium bowl. Mix until well
combined. Sprinkle a little over the cupcakes before baking them.

walnut & cinnamon-frosted banana cupcakes
Prepare the basic cupcake recipe. Add 3 tablespoons chopped walnuts and
1 teaspoon cinnamon to the frosting after creaming it.

madeleines

see base recipe page 40

cassis-frosted madeleines
Prepare the basic recipe. For the frosting, add 3 tablespoons cassis liqueur
to the creamed butter and sugar.

chocolate madeleines
Prepare the basic recipe. Substitute 2 tablespoons Dutch-process cocoa
powder for 2 tablespoons of the flour.

vanilla madeleines
Prepare the basic recipe. Add 1 teaspoon vanilla extract to the eggs and
sugar before creaming the batter. Add 1 teaspoon vanilla extract to the
sugar, butter, salt, and orange zest before creaming the frosting.

fragrant & spiced cupcakes

Exotic and unexpected flavors make these cupcakes a culinary

adventure. Unusual pairings — pistachio and rosewater, fig and

vanilla, cardamom and orange — abound.

carnation cupcakes

see variations page 78

Cooking with flowers goes back centuries. You can find old recipes for flower water, jellies, jams, and yes, cupcakes!

for the cupcakes
1 cup (2 sticks) sweet butter, softened
1 cup superfine sugar
2 cups self-rising flour
4 eggs
1 tsp. vanilla extract

for the frosting
1 3/4 cups confectioners' sugar
2 tbsp. lemon juice
3 dozen red, pink, or striped carnations

Preheat the oven to 350°F (175°C). Place 18 paper baking cups in muffin pans. Combine all the cupcake ingredients in a large bowl and beat with an electric mixer until smooth and pale, about 2 to 3 minutes. Spoon the batter into the cups. Bake for 20 minutes. Remove pans from the oven and cool for 5 minutes. Then remove the cupcakes and cool on a rack.

To make the frosting, sift the confectioners' sugar into a medium bowl. Slowly add the lemon juice, stirring until the frosting holds its shape. Spread the frosting onto the cooled cupcakes. Snip the heels off the carnation flowers and place a flower in the center of each cupcake.

Store in an airtight container for up to 3 days, or freeze unfrosted in an airtight container for up to 3 months.

Makes 1 1/2 dozen

chai cupcakes

see variations page 79

Chai is a spiced Indian tea made with frothy warm milk — almost like an Indian cappuccino! This cupcake captures its light, spicy flavor.

for the cupcakes
2 cups self-rising flour
1/4 tsp. baking powder
Pinch of salt
1 tbsp. chai tea powder
1/4 cup (1/2 stick) sweet butter, softened
3/4 cup packed light brown sugar
2 egg whites
2/3 cup buttermilk

for the frosting
1 cup cream cheese, softened
1 1/2 cups confectioners' sugar, sifted
1 tbsp. lemon juice
1 tsp. vanilla extract

Preheat the oven to 350°F (175°C). Place 12 baking cups in a muffin pan. In a medium bowl, mix the flour, baking powder, salt, and chai powder. In a separate bowl, beat the butter and sugar until smooth. Add the egg whites slowly, beating well. Slowly add the flour mixture, and finally the buttermilk. Mix until combined. Spoon the batter into the cups. Bake for 20 minutes. Remove pan from the oven and cool for 5 minutes. Then remove the cupcakes and cool on a rack. To make the frosting, mix the cream cheese and confectioners' sugar together in a medium bowl and beat until soft and light. Add the lemon and vanilla, and beat until smooth. Spoon the frosting over the cupcakes. Store unfrosted in an airtight container for up to 3 days, or freeze for up to 3 months.

Makes 1 dozen

fennel cupcakes

see variations page 80

Lightly crushed fennel seeds give this cupcake a sweet licorice flavor. In India, they are chewed after meals to refresh the breath.

for the cupcakes
1 cup (2 sticks) sweet butter, softened
1 cup superfine sugar
2 cups self-rising flour
4 eggs
1 tsp. finely crushed fennel seeds

for the frosting
1 cup cream cheese, softened
1 1/2 cups confectioners' sugar, sifted
1 tbsp. licorice-flavored liqueur
1 tsp. vanilla extract
1 tsp. lightly crushed fennel seeds

Preheat the oven to 350°F (175°C). Place 18 paper baking cups in muffin pans. Combine all the cupcake ingredients in a medium bowl and beat with an electric mixer until smooth and pale, about 2 to 3 minutes. Spoon the batter into the cups. Bake for 20 minutes. Remove pans from the oven and cool for 5 minutes. Then remove the cupcakes and cool on a rack.

To make the frosting, combine the cream cheese and confectioners' sugar, and beat briskly until soft and creamy. Add the liqueur and vanilla, and stir well. Swirl onto the top of the cupcakes, and decorate with the fennel seeds.

Store unfrosted for up to 3 days in an airtight container, or freeze for 3 months.

Makes 1 1/2 dozen

rhubarb & ginger cupcakes

see variations page 81

The combination of rhubarb and ginger is magnificent. It is believed that rhubarb originated in China, where it was used for its medicinal properties.

for the cupcakes
1 cup (2 sticks) sweet butter, softened
1 cup superfine sugar
2 cups self-rising flour
4 eggs
1 tsp. vanilla extract
1 cup cooked rhubarb

for the frosting
1 cup cream cheese, softened
1 1/2 cups confectioners' sugar, sifted
1 tbsp. lime juice
1/2 tsp. ground ginger
1 1/2 tbsp. roughly chopped candied ginger

Preheat the oven to 400°F (200°C). Place 18 paper baking cups in muffin pans. Combine all the cupcake ingredients, except the rhubarb, in a medium bowl and beat with an electric mixer until smooth and pale, about 2 to 3 minutes. Spoon the batter into the cups. Bake for 20 minutes. Remove pans from the oven and cool for 5 minutes. Then remove the cupcakes and cool on a rack. Hollow out a small hole in each cake and fill with 1 teaspoon rhubarb.

For the frosting, combine the cream cheese and confectioners' sugar, and beat briskly until soft and creamy. Add the lime juice, ground ginger, and candied ginger and mix well. Spoon onto the cupcakes.

Store unfrosted in an airtight container for up to 3 days, or freeze for up to 3 months.

Makes 1 1/2 dozen

lavender & honey cupcakes

see variations page 82

The marriage of lavender and honey is truly wonderful. If you can find lavender honey, it will enhance the flavor even more.

for the cupcakes
1 cup (2 sticks) sweet butter, softened
1 cup superfine sugar
2 cups self-rising flour
4 eggs
1 tsp. vanilla extract

for the frosting
1 cup cream cheese, softened
1 1/2 cups confectioners' sugar, sifted
1/3 cup honey
Blue food coloring
2 tbsp. dried lavender flowers

Preheat the oven to 400°F (200°C). Place 18 baking cups in muffin pans. Combine all the cupcake ingredients in a medium bowl and beat with an electric mixer until smooth and pale, about 2 to 3 minutes. Spoon the batter into the cups. Bake for 20 minutes. Remove pans from the oven and cool for 5 minutes. Then remove the cupcakes and cool on a rack.

For the frosting, beat the cream cheese and confectioners' sugar in a medium bowl with an electric mixer, until light and creamy. Beat in the honey and a few drops of the food coloring. Stir in half of the lavender flowers.

Spread the frosting onto the cupcakes and sprinkle with the reserved lavender flowers.

Store without frosting in an airtight container for up to 3 days, or freeze for up to 3 months.

Makes 1 1/2 dozen

hummingbird cupcakes with marmalade frosting

see variations page 83

The hummingbird cake is a classic recipe from the American South.

for the cupcakes
1 1/4 cups all-purpose flour
1 tsp. baking powder
1/2 tsp. cinnamon
3/4 cup superfine sugar
1/2 cup safflower oil
2 eggs
1/2 cup (2 medium) mashed bananas
1 1/2 tbsp. grated orange zest

1/2 cup shredded carrot
1/2 cup crushed pineapple, drained
1/2 cup (2 oz.) flaked coconut

for the frosting
1/2 cup (1 stick) sweet butter, softened
2 1/2 cups confectioners' sugar, sifted
2 tbsp. freshly squeezed orange juice
2 tbsp. orange marmalade

Preheat the oven to 350°F (175°C). Place 12 baking cups in a muffin pan. In a medium bowl, sift the flour, baking powder, and cinnamon. In a large bowl cream the sugar and oil with an electric mixer until light and fluffy. Beat in the eggs slowly, then stir in the dry ingredients in 3 batches. Add the rest of the ingredients, and stir until combined. Spoon the batter into the cups. Bake for 25 minutes. Remove pan from the oven and cool for 5 minutes. Then remove the cupcakes and cool on a rack. To make the frosting, beat the butter in a medium bowl. Add the remaining ingredients. Smear the frosting onto the cupcakes. Store unfrosted in an airtight container for up to 3 days, or freeze for up to 3 months.

Makes 1 dozen

pistachio & rosewater cupcakes

see variations page 84

Rosewater is a delicate, sweet flavoring made by steeping rose petals in water, oil, or alcohol. Try to use unsalted pistachios for this recipe.

for the cupcakes
1 cup (2 sticks) sweet butter, softened
1 cup superfine sugar
2 cups self-rising flour
4 eggs
1 tsp. rosewater

for the frosting
1 cup cream cheese
1 1/2 cups confectioners' sugar, sifted
2 tbsp. rosewater
3 tbsp. pistachios, chopped

Preheat the oven to 350°F (175°C). Place 18 paper baking cups in muffin pans. Combine all the cupcake ingredients in a medium bowl and beat with an electric mixer until smooth and pale, about 2 to 3 minutes.

Spoon the batter into the cups. Bake for 20 minutes. Remove pans from the oven and cool for 5 minutes. Then remove the cupcakes and cool on a rack.

For the frosting, combine the cream cheese and confectioners' sugar, and beat with an electric mixer until soft and creamy. Add the rosewater and pistachios, and stir well. Swirl onto the top of the cupcakes.

Store without frosting for up to 3 days in an airtight container, or freeze for up to 3 months.

Makes 1 dozen

orange & armagnac cupcakes

see variations page 85

For adults only! These cupcakes would be ideal on a cold winter night.

for the cupcakes
1 cup (2 sticks) sweet butter, softened
1 cup superfine sugar
2 cups self-rising flour
4 eggs
2 tbsp. Armagnac

for the frosting
1 cup cream cheese, softened
1 1/2 cups confectioners' sugar, sifted
1 tsp. orange extract
1 1/2 tbsp. grated orange zest

Preheat the oven to 350°F (175°C). Place 18 paper baking cups in muffin pans. Combine all the cupcake ingredients in a medium bowl and beat with an electric mixer until smooth and pale, about 2 to 3 minutes. Spoon the batter into the cups.

Bake for 20 minutes. Remove pans from the oven and cool for 5 minutes. Pierce some holes in the tops of the cupcakes with a skewer and pour 1/2 tablespoon Armagnac over each. Then remove the cupcakes and cool on a rack.

To make the frosting, beat the cream cheese in a bowl with an electric mixer until light and fluffy. Beat in the confectioners' sugar for 1 to 2 minutes, then beat in the orange extract and zest until smooth and light. Spread the frosting on the cupcakes.

Store unfrosted for up to 2 days in an airtight container, or freeze for up to 3 months.

Makes 1 1/2 dozen

spiced sour cream cupcakes

see variations page 86

The hearty flavor of these cupcakes are perfect for tailgating parties and fall picnics.

for the cupcakes
1 1/2 cups all-purpose flour
1 tsp. baking powder
2 tsp. cinnamon
1 tsp. allspice
1/4 tsp. nutmeg
2 eggs
3/4 cup sour cream
1 cup packed light brown sugar

3 tbsp. golden raisins
3 tbsp. chopped pecans

for the frosting
1 cup cream cheese, softened
1/2 cup (1 stick) sweet butter, softened
1 1/2 cups confectioners' sugar, sifted
1 tbsp. grated orange zest
2 tbsp. orange juice

Preheat the oven to 350°F (175°C). Place 18 paper baking cups in muffin pans. Sift the dry ingredients into a medium bowl and put aside. In a large bowl, beat the eggs and sour cream with an electric mixer. Add the sugar and mix well. Then add the dry ingredients in 3 batches, and mix until smooth. Stir in the raisins and pecans. Spoon the batter into the cups. Bake for 20 minutes until firm. Remove pans from the oven and cool for 5 minutes. Then remove the cupcakes and cool on a rack. To make the frosting, beat the cream cheese and butter together with an electric mixer, until light and fluffy. Add the confectioners' sugar and beat until creamy. Beat in the orange zest and the juice. Spread the frosting on the cupcakes.

Store unfrosted in an airtight container for up to 3 days, or freeze for up to 3 months.

Makes 1 1/2 dozen

cardamom & orange cupcakes

see variations page 87

Cardamom has a pungent aroma and is often used in Indian cooking to flavor curries.

for the cupcakes
1 cup (2 sticks) sweet butter, softened
1 cup superfine sugar
2 cups self-rising flour
4 eggs
1 tsp. ground cardamom
1 tsp. orange extract

for the frosting
2 cups confectioners' sugar, sifted
1/2 cup (1 stick) sweet butter, softened
1/4 cup sour cream
1 1/2 tbsp. grated orange zest
1 tsp. orange extract
36 cardamom pods (for decoration only)

Preheat the oven to 350°F (175°C). Place 18 paper baking cups in muffin pans. Combine all the cupcake ingredients in a medium bowl and beat with an electric mixer until smooth and pale, about 2 to 3 minutes.

Spoon the batter into the cups. Bake in the oven for 20 minutes. Remove pans from the oven and cool for 5 minutes. Then remove the cupcakes and cool on a rack.

To make the frosting, beat the confectioners' sugar, butter, sour cream, orange zest, and orange extract with an electric mixer until smooth. Spread the frosting on the cupcakes and top each with 2 cardamom pods. Store unfrosted for up to 2 days in an airtight container, or freeze for up to 3 months.

Makes 1 1/2 dozen

zucchini & feta muffins

see variations page 88

These savory muffins offer a flavor from the Mediterranean. You'll find zucchini and feta combined in Greek and Turkish salads, alongside plump olives and flatbreads.

2 cups all-purpose flour
1 tbsp. baking powder
Pinch of salt
2 eggs
1/2 cup virgin olive oil

1 1/2 cups (about 2 or 3 medium) shredded
  zucchini
1 cup crumbled feta cheese
1 1/2 tbsp. grated lemon zest

Preheat the oven to 350°F (175°C). Grease a 6-cup muffin pan.

Sift the dry ingredients together in a medium bowl. In a large bowl, beat the eggs and oil with an electric mixer until smooth.

Stir in the zucchini, feta cheese, and lemon zest. Add the dry ingredients, and stir until the mixture is just combined.

Spoon the mixture into the prepared pan. Bake for 30 minutes. Remove pan from the oven and cool for 5 minutes. Remove the muffins and cool on a rack.

Store refrigerated in an airtight container for up to 2 days, or freeze for up to 3 months.

Makes 1/2 dozen

fig & vanilla cupcakes

see variations page 89

Dried figs are sweeter than fresh figs. Indeed, the Romans used dried figs as sweetners because cane sugar was so rare and expensive.

for the cupcakes
1 cup (2 sticks) sweet butter, softened
1 cup superfine sugar
2 cups self-rising flour
1 tsp. baking powder
4 eggs
1 tbsp. vanilla extract
1 cup (5 oz.) finely chopped, dried figs

for the frosting
1 cup cream cheese, softened
1 1/2 cups confectioners' sugar, sifted
1 tsp. vanilla extract
1 tbsp. grated lemon zest
3 tbsp. chopped figs

Preheat the oven to 350°F (175°C). Place 18 baking cups in muffin pans. Combine all the cupcake ingredients in a large bowl and beat with an electric mixer until smooth and pale, about 2 to 3 minutes.

Spoon the batter into the cups. Bake for 20 minutes. Remove pans from the oven and cool for 5 minutes. Then remove the cupcakes and cool on a rack.

To make the frosting, beat the cream cheese, confectioners' sugar, vanilla, and lemon zest with an electric mixer until soft and creamy. Smear the cupcakes with the frosting. Store unfrosted in an airtight container for up to 2 days, or freeze for up to 3 months.

Makes 1 1/2 dozen

carnation cupcakes

see base recipe page 57

frosted flower cupcakes
Prepare the basic cupcake recipe. To prepare the frosted flowers, put an egg white in a small bowl and some granulated sugar in another small bowl. Take a selection of flower petals (roses and pansies work well) and brush with egg white on both sides. Dust the petals with the sugar, place on a tray, and leave in a cool dry place to dry and stiffen. Lay on top of the frosted cupcakes.

rose cupcakes
Prepare the basic cupcake recipe. Substitute 2 dozen rose petals for the carnations.

citrus cream carnation cupcakes
Prepare the basic cupcake recipe. To make a citrus cream frosting, combine 1/2 cup cream cheese with 2 teaspoons orange and lemon zest in a small bowl. Stir in 3 tablespoons confectioners' sugar, spread onto the cupcakes, and garnish with the carnations.

variations

chai cupcakes

see base recipe page 58

chocolate chip & chai cupcakes
Prepare the basic cupcake recipe, stirring in 1/2 cup (3 1/2 oz.) semisweet
chocolate chips after adding the buttermilk.

cinnamon & orange chai cupcakes
Prepare the basic cupcake recipe, adding 2 teaspoons cinnamon to the dry
ingredients. Add 1 tablespoon grated orange zest along with the buttermilk.

white chocolate & vanilla chai cupcakes
Prepare the basic cupcake recipe. Add 1/2 cup (3 1/2 oz.) white chocolate
chips and 1 teaspoon vanilla extract after adding the buttermilk.

variations

fennel cupcakes

see base recipe page 61

fennel & orange cupcakes
Prepare the basic cupcake recipe. Add 1 tablespoon finely grated orange zest to the cupcake mixture. For the frosting, substitute 1 teaspoon orange extract for the vanilla.

fennel & almond cupcakes
Prepare the basic cupcake recipe, adding 4 tablespoons chopped blanched almonds after mixing the cupcake batter.

fennel & pink pepper cupcakes
Prepare the basic cupcake recipe. For the frosting, omit the vanilla extract and instead add 1 teaspoon finely crushed pink peppercorns.

rhubarb & ginger cupcakes

see base recipe page 62

rhubarb & cinnamon cupcakes
Prepare the basic cupcake recipe. Add 2 teaspoons cinnamon to the cupcake mixture before stirring the batter.

rhubarb & custard cupcakes
Prepare the basic cupcake recipe. Slice the cupcakes horizontally and spread 1 tablespoon custard (or prepared vanilla pudding) onto the base. Pop the top back on and smother with the ginger frosting.

golden raisin, rhubarb, & ginger cupcakes
Prepare the basic cupcake recipe. After mixing the batter, add 1/4 cup (2 oz.) golden raisins.

lavender & honey cupcakes

see base recipe page 65

bitter chocolate & lavender cupcakes

Prepare the basic cupcake recipe. After mixing the batter, fold
in 1/2 cup (3 1/2 oz.) semisweet chocolate chips.

gumdrop & lavender cupcakes

Prepare the basic cupcake recipe. After mixing the batter, fold
in 1/2 cup (3 1/2 oz.) mixed fruit gumdrops to the batter.

lavender & orange flower cream cupcakes

Prepare the basic cupcake recipe. To make the frosting, combine
3 tablespoons orange flower water with the cream cheese and
confectioners' sugar. Beat well and stir in the lavender flowers.

hummingbird cupcakes with marmalade frosting

see base recipe page 66

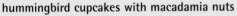

hummingbird cupcakes with macadamia nuts
Prepare the basic cupcake recipe adding 1/2 cup (3 1/2 oz.) chopped macadamia nuts after mixing in the eggs.

hummingbird cupcakes with figs
Prepare the basic cupcake recipe, substituting 1/4 cup (2 oz.) chopped dried figs for the pineapple.

hummingird cupcakes with lemon frosting
Prepare the basic cupcake recipe. To make the frosting, substitute 2 tablespoons lemon juice for the orange juice, and 2 tablespoons lemon curd for the marmalade.

variations

pistachio & rosewater cupcakes

see base recipe page 69

pomegranate & rosewater cupcakes
Prepare the basic cupcake recipe. For the frosting, add
3 tablespoons pomegranate seeds after combining the
cream cheese and confectioners' sugar.

walnut & rosewater cupcakes
Prepare the basic cupcake recipe. For the frosting, substitute
3 tablespoons chopped walnuts for the pistachios.

almond & rosewater cupcakes
Prepare the basic cupcake recipe. For the frosting, substitute
3 tablespoons toasted almonds for the pistachios.

variations

orange & armagnac cupcakes

see base recipe page 70

chocolate chip & armagnac cupcakes
Prepare the basic cupcake recipe, adding 1/2 cup (3 1/2 oz.) semisweet chocolate chips after combining the rest of the cupcake ingredients.

almond & amaretto cupcakes
Prepare the basic cupcake recipe, substituting 2 tablespoons Amaretto for the Armagnac. Add 3 tablespoons ground almonds to the cupcake mixture along with the other ingredients. For the frosting, add 2 tablespoons chopped almonds, and omit the orange juice and zest.

hazelnut & kahlua cupcakes
Prepare the basic cupcake recipe, substituting 2 tablespoons Kahlua for the Armagnac. Add 3 tablespoons finely chopped hazelnuts to the cupcake mixture along with the other ingredients. For the frosting, add 2 tablespoons chopped hazelnuts, and omit the orange juice and zest.

variations

spiced sour cream cupcakes

see base recipe page 71

ginger-frosted spiced cupcakes
Prepare the basic cupcake recipe. For the frosting, substitute 3 tablespoons chopped candied ginger for the orange zest and orange juice.

coffee-frosted spiced cupcakes
Prepare the basic cupcake recipe. To make the frosting, mix 2 tablespoons strong coffee and 2 tablespoons malted milk powder until dissolved. Whisk 1 1/2 cups confectioners' sugar into the coffee mixture until dissolved.

maple & walnut-frosted spiced cupcakes
Prepare the basic cupcake recipe. To make the frosting, add 1/2 teaspoon maple-flavored extract to the creamed confectioners' sugar, butter, and cream cheese. Omit the orange juice and zest. Smear the frosting onto the cupcakes and top with 1/2 cup (3 1/2 oz.) chopped walnuts.

cardamom & orange cupcakes

see base recipe page 73

coffee & cardamom-frosted cupcakes

Prepare the basic cupcake recipe. For the frosting, omit the orange zest
and extract. Add 2 tablespoons instant coffee granules to 1 teaspoon hot
coffee. Stir to dissolve. Stir in 1 tablespoon Kahlua. Set aside to cool. Stir
the cooled coffee mixture into the creamed confectioners' sugar, butter,
and sour cream.

cardamom custard cupcakes

Prepare the basic cupcake recipe. Slice the cupcakes horizontally and
spread 1 tablespoon custard (or prepared vanilla pudding) onto the base.
Pop the top back on and smother with the orange frosting.

cardamom & lemongrass cupcakes

Prepare the basic cupcake recipe. For the frosting, add 1 tablespoon
finely chopped lemongrass after creaming the other ingredients.

variations

zucchini & feta muffins

see base recipe page 74

carrot & zucchini muffins
Prepare the basic muffin recipe, substituting 3/4 cup finely shredded carrot for 3/4 cup shredded zucchini.

zucchini, feta, & olive muffins
Prepare the basic muffin recipe, adding 3 tablespoons finely chopped olives to the muffin batter.

orange & zucchini muffins
Prepare the basic muffin recipe, adding 1 tablespoon finely grated orange zest to the muffin batter.

variations

fig & vanilla cupcakes

see base recipe page 77

orange-frosted fig & vanilla cupcakes
Prepare the basic cupcake recipe. In the frosting, add 2 tablespoons orange marmalade and substitute 1 tablespoon orange zest for the lemon zest.

fig & vanilla cupcakes with honey buttercream
Prepare the basic cupcake recipe. For the frosting, add 1/3 cup honey after combining the cream cheese and confectioners' sugar.

ginger-frosted fig & vanilla cupcakes
Prepare the basic cupcake recipe. For the frosting, add 1 teaspoon ground ginger and 1/4 cup (2 oz.) candied ginger after combining the cream cheese and confectioners' sugar.

chocolate cupcakes

Minted chocolate cupcakes, chocolate chip and raisin brioches,

white chocolate and strawberry cupcakes — the cupcakes in this

chapter will satisfy your chocolate craving in an instant!

chocolate mud cupcakes

see variations page 111

These cupcakes are so simple to make you won't hesitate to make another batch!

1 cup (7 oz.) semisweet chocolate chips
1 1/3 cups (2 1/2 sticks) sweet butter
5 eggs

2/3 cup superfine sugar
3/4 cup self-rising flour
2 tbsp. Dutch-process cocoa powder, for dusting

Preheat the oven to 325°F (160°C). Place 12 paper baking cups in a muffin pan.

In a double boiler, or a medium bowl set over a pan of gently simmering water, melt the chocolate and butter together, stirring well. Leave to cool a little.

Beat the eggs and sugar in a large bowl until pale and thick. Fold the flour into the egg mixture and then stir in the melted chocolate and butter until well blended.

Spoon the mixture into the cups and bake for 20 minutes. The cupcakes will be soft and gooey in texture and appearance. Remove pan from the oven and cool for 5 minutes. Then remove the cupcakes from pan. Serve swiftly, dusted with cocoa powder.

Store in the refrigerator in an airtight container for up to 3 days.

Makes 1 dozen

chocolate ice cream cupcakes

see variations page 112

It's best to move these cupcakes from freezer to refrigerator 30 minutes before serving.

for the cupcakes
1 cup (2 sticks) sweet butter, softened
1 cup superfine sugar
1 1/2 cups self-rising flour
4 tbsp. Dutch-process cocoa powder
1 tsp. baking powder
4 eggs
1 tsp. vanilla extract

for the filling and glaze
1 cup chocolate ice cream
1/2 cup (3 1/2 oz.) semisweet chocolate chips
1/3 cup heavy cream

Preheat the oven to 350°F (175°C). Place 18 paper baking cups in muffin pans. Combine all the cupcake ingredients in a medium bowl and beat with an electric mixer until smooth and creamy, about 2 to 3 minutes.

Spoon the batter into the cups. Bake for 20 minutes. Remove pans from the oven and cool for 5 minutes. Then remove the cupcakes and cool on a rack. When cool, slice the cupcakes horizontally and spread a little softened ice cream on the bottom slice. Place the top back on the cupcake and freeze. Prepare the glaze by melting the chocolate in a double boiler, or a medium bowl over a pan of simmering water, stirring until completely melted. Remove from the heat. Add the cream and stir until well combined. Cool slightly and spoon over the cupcakes. Return to the freezer to set. Freeze in an airtight container for up to 3 months.

Makes 1 1/2 dozen

chocolate brownie cupcakes

see variations page 113

Serve these warm from the oven, topped with a generous spoonful of vanilla cream.

for the cupcakes
3/4 cup (4 1/2 oz.) semisweet chocolate chips
1/2 cup (1 stick) sweet butter
2 eggs
1 1/2 cups superfine sugar
1 tsp. vanilla extract
1 cup all-purpose flour

for the topping
1 cup heavy cream
1 tsp. vanilla extract
3 tbsp. confectioners' sugar, sifted

Preheat the oven to 325°F (160°C). Place 12 paper baking cups in a muffin pan. Melt the chocolate and butter in a double boiler or medium bowl set over a pan of simmering water, stirring until melted. Set aside to cool. In a medium bowl, beat the eggs, sugar, and vanilla until pale and thick. Fold in the chocolate and then the flour, mixing until well combined.

Spoon batter into the cups. Bake for 25 minutes. Remove pan from the oven and cool for 5 minutes. Then remove the cupcakes and cool on a rack.

For the topping, beat the cream in a medium bowl until semi-stiff. Fold in the vanilla and confectioners' sugar. Place a dollop or two on each brownie.

Store without topping in an airtight container for up to 2 days.

Makes 1 dozen

white chocolate & strawberry cupcakes

see variations page 114

Simple yet sophisticated — and perfect for a summer picnic!

for the cupcakes
1 cup (2 sticks) sweet butter, softened
1 cup superfine sugar
2 cups self-rising flour
1 tsp. baking powder
4 eggs
1 tsp. strawberry extract
1/2 cup (3 1/2 oz.) white chocolate chips

for the frosting
1 cup cream cheese, softened
1 1/2 cups confectioners' sugar, sifted
1 tsp. vanilla extract
3 tbsp. sweet butter, softened
3 tbsp. chopped fresh strawberries

Preheat the oven to 350°F (175°C). Place 18 paper baking cups in muffin pans. Combine the butter, sugar, flour, baking powder, eggs, and strawberry extract in a medium bowl. Beat with an electric mixer until light and creamy, about 2 to 3 minutes. Stir in the chocolate chips. Spoon the batter into the cups. Bake for 20 minutes. Remove pans from the oven and cool for 5 minutes. Then remove the cupcakes and cool on a rack. To make the frosting, beat the cream cheese, confectioners' sugar, vanilla, and butter until smooth and creamy. Stir in the chopped strawberries. Spread frosting on top of the cupcakes.

Store unfrosted in an airtight container for up to 2 days, or freeze for up to 3 months.

Makes 1 1/2 dozen

chocolate & chili cupcakes

see variations page 115

The Spanish *conquistadors* brought chocolate back from Mexico, a fact that inspired this delicious combination of bittersweet chocolate and tingling chili.

for the cupcakes
1 cup (2 sticks) sweet butter, softened
1 cup superfine sugar
1 1/2 cups self-rising flour
4 tbsp. Dutch-process cocoa powder
1 tsp. baking powder
4 eggs
2 tsp. chipotle chili powder
1/2 cup (3 1/2 oz.) semisweet chocolate chips

for the frosting
1 1/2 cups confectioners' sugar, sifted
1/2 cup Dutch-process cocoa powder
3 tbsp. Tia Maria
1/2 cup (1 stick) sweet butter, softened

Preheat the oven to 350°F (175°C). Place 18 paper baking cups in muffin pans. Combine all the cupcake ingredients, except the chocolate chips, in a large bowl and beat with an electric mixer until smooth, about 2 to 3 minutes. Stir in the chocolate chips.

Spoon the batter into the cups. Bake for 20 minutes. Remove pans from the oven and cool for 5 minutes. Then remove the cupcakes and cool on a rack.

To make the frosting, blend all the ingredients together in a food processor. Spread the frosting on the cooled cupcakes. Store unfrosted in an airtight container for up to 2 days.

Makes 1 1/2 dozen

white chocolate &
macadamia nut cupcakes

see variations page 116

Technically, white chocolate is not a chocolate, but it tastes just as decadent!

for the cupcakes
1 cup (2 sticks) sweet butter, softened
1 cup superfine sugar
2 cups self-rising flour
1 tsp. baking powder
4 eggs
1 tsp. vanilla extract
1/2 cup (3 1/2 oz.) white chocolate chips

for the frosting
1 cup (7 oz.) white chocolate chips
5 tbsp. milk
1 1/2 cups confectioners' sugar, sifted
3 tbsp. chopped, toasted macadamia nuts

Preheat the oven to 350°F (175°C). Place 18 paper baking cups in muffin pans. Combine all the cupcake ingredients, except the chocolate chips, in a large bowl and beat with an electric mixer until smooth and pale, about 2 to 3 minutes. Stir in the chocolate chips. Spoon the batter into the cups. Bake for 20 minutes. Remove pans from the oven and cool for 5 minutes. Then remove the cupcakes and cool on a rack. To make the frosting, melt the chocolate and milk in a double boiler, stirring frequently. Remove from the heat and beat in the confectioners' sugar until smooth. Spread over the cupcakes and sprinkle with the nuts.

Store in an airtight container for up to 2 days.

Makes 1 1/2 dozen

choc fudge-frosted cupcakes

see variations page 117

This fudge frosting is bound to bring even the mildest chocaholics to their knees!

for the cupcakes
1 cup (2 sticks) sweet butter, softened
1 cup superfine sugar
2 cups self-rising flour
1 tsp. baking powder
4 eggs
1 tsp. vanilla extract

for the frosting
3 1/2 oz. semisweet chocolate, roughly chopped
2 tbsp. milk
1/4 cup (1/2 stick) sweet butter
3/4 cup confectioners' sugar, sifted

Preheat the oven to 350°F (175°C). Place 18 paper baking cups into muffin pans. Combine all the cupcake ingredients in a medium bowl and beat with an electric mixer until smooth and pale, about 2 to 3 minutes. Spoon the batter into the cups. Bake for 20 minutes. Remove the pans from the oven and cool for 5 minutes. Remove the cupcakes and cool on the rack.

To make the frosting, gently heat the chocolate, milk, and butter in a small, heavy saucepan, stirring until melted. Remove from the heat and beat in the confectioners' sugar.

Swirl the frosting onto the cooled cupcakes.

Store unfrosted in an airtight container for up to 3 days, or freeze for up to 3 months.

Makes 1 1/2 dozen

devil's food cupcakes

see variations page 118

These cupcakes are incredibly rich and moist delights!

for the cupcakes
2 cups self-rising flour
1 tsp. baking powder
1 cup packed light brown sugar
1 cup (2 sticks) sweet butter, softened
2 separated eggs
3 1/2 oz. semisweet chocolate, melted
1 tsp. vanilla extract
1/2 cup milk

for the frosting
1/2 cup (1 stick) sweet butter, softened
1 tbsp. milk
3 1/2 oz. semisweet chocolate, melted
1 tsp. vanilla extract
3/4 cup confectioners' sugar, sifted

Preheat the oven to 350°F (175°C). Place 18 paper baking cups into muffin pans. Sift the flour and baking powder and set aside. In a medium bowl, cream the sugar and butter. Add the egg yolks and beat well. Add the melted chocolate and vanilla, mixing well. Add the flour and milk alternately, beating well with each addition. Beat the egg whites in a medium bowl until soft peaks form, and gently fold them into the batter.

Spoon the batter into the cups. Bake for 20 minutes. Remove pans from the oven and cool for 5 minutes. Then remove the cupcakes and cool on a rack. To make the frosting, cream the butter in a medium bowl. Beat in the milk until smooth. Stir in the chocolate and vanilla. Beat in the confectioners' sugar until thick and creamy. Spread over the cupcakes. Store unfrosted in an airtight container for up to 2 days, or freeze for up to 3 months.

Makes 1 1/2 dozen

choc 'n' cherry cupcakes

see variations page 119

The classic German dessert "Black Forest Cake" was the inspiration for this cupcake.

for the cupcakes
1 1/2 cups self-rising flour
4 tbsp. Dutch-process cocoa powder
1 tsp. baking powder
1 cup superfine sugar
1 cup (2 sticks) sweet butter, softened
4 eggs
1/2 cup chopped cherries
2 tbsp. kirsch (or other cherry-flavored liqueur)

for the topping
3/4 cup heavy cream
3 tbsp. confectioners' sugar, sifted
12 whole cherries
3 1/2 oz. semisweet chocolate bar

Preheat the oven to 325°F (160°C). Place 18 paper baking cups in muffin pans. In a medium bowl, sift together the flour, cocoa, and baking powder. Set aside. Cream the sugar and butter in a large bowl until smooth. Add the eggs one at a time, beating well with each addition. Add the flour mixture and the cherries, and stir until well combined. Spoon the batter into the cups. Bake for 20 minutes. Remove pans from the oven and cool for 5 minutes. Pour a little kirsch over each cupcake. Remove the cupcakes from the pans and cool on a rack. For the topping, whip the cream and confectioners' sugar together until slightly stiff. Using a vegetable peeler, shave curls of chocolate from the bar. Garnish the cupcakes with a dollop of cream. Place a cherry in the center and chocolate around it. Store unfrosted in an airtight container for up to 3 days.

Makes 1 1/2 dozen

mint chocolate cupcakes

see variations page 120

Mint is a versatile herb that complements both sweet and savory dishes.

for the cupcakes
1 1/2 cups self-rising flour
4 tbsp. Dutch-process cocoa powder
1 tsp. baking powder
1 cup superfine sugar
1 cup (2 sticks) sweet butter, softened
4 eggs
1 tsp. mint extract
1/2 cup (3 1/2 oz.) semisweet chocolate chips

for the frosting
1/3 cup (2/3 stick) sweet butter, softened
2 cups confectioners' sugar, sifted
1 tsp. mint extract
Green food coloring
1/2 cup (3 1/2 oz.) semisweet chocolate chips

Preheat the oven to 325°F (160°C). Place 18 paper baking cups into muffin pans. In a medium bowl, sift together the flour, cocoa, and baking powder. Set aside. Beat the sugar and butter together in a large bowl until smooth. Add the eggs one at a time, beating well after each addition. Add the flour mixture gradually, stirring until well combined. Stir in the mint extract and chocolate chips. Spoon the mixture into the cups. Bake for 20 minutes. Remove the pans from the oven and cool for 5 minutes. Then remove the cupcakes and cool on a rack. To make the frosting, beat the butter and confectioners' sugar in a small bowl until smooth and creamy. Stir in the mint extract and just enough food coloring to turn the frosting a mint green. Frost the cupcakes and decorate with chocolate chips. Store unfrosted in an airtight container for up to 3 days, or freeze for up to 3 months.

Makes 1 1/2 dozen

chocolate chip & raisin brioches

see variations page 121

You'll find yourself drawn to the breakfast table by the aroma of these sweet breads, a perfect accompaniment to steaming hot coffee.

1/2 tbsp. active dry yeast
1/2 cup warm water
1 tsp. sugar
2 1/2 cups all-purpose flour
4 eggs
1/4 cup superfine sugar

Pinch of salt
1/2 cup (1 stick) sweet butter, softened
1/2 cup (3 1/2 oz.) raisins
1/2 cup (3 1/2 oz.) semisweet chocolate chips
1 beaten egg

Combine the yeast, water, and the teaspoon of sugar in a large bowl. Stir well and leave in a warm place for 10 minutes. Stir in 1/2 cup of the flour until the mixture becomes a smooth paste. Beat the eggs and add them to the yeast mixture. Add the sugar and salt. Stir in the remaining flour, and mix until the dough is soft and slightly sticky. Leave in a warm place, covered with plastic wrap, for 45 minutes or until doubled in bulk. Preheat the oven to 400°F (200°C). Grease 12 mini brioche or muffin molds. Beat in the butter, raisins, and chocolate chips. Fill the molds halfway. Leave in a warm place to rise for about 20 minutes, until the dough has risen to fill about two-thirds each mold.

Brush each brioche with a little of the beaten egg and bake for 20 minutes. Cool in the molds for 5 minutes, remove, and cool on a rack. Store in an airtight container for up to 2 days.

Makes 1 dozen

chocolate hazelnut cupcakes

see variations page 122

A timeless combination . . . with very little flour in the mix!

1/2 cup (1 stick) sweet butter
1/2 cup (3 1/2 oz.) semisweet chocolate chips
1/2 cup superfine sugar

4 separated eggs
2 tbsp. all-purpose flour
1/2 cup (1 1/2 oz.) chopped, roasted hazelnuts

Preheat the oven to 325°F (160°C). Place 12 paper baking cups in a muffin pan. Melt the butter and chocolate in a double boiler, or medium bowl over a pan of simmering water, stirring until completely melted. Cool slightly.

Beat the sugar and egg yolks in a medium bowl until thick and creamy. Stir the butter and chocolate, flour, and hazelnuts into the egg mixture.

In a medium bowl, beat the egg whites to soft peaks, and gently fold into the chocolate mixture. Spoon the batter into the cups. Bake for 20 minutes. Remove pan from the oven and cool for 5 minutes. Then remove the cupcakes and cool on a rack.

Store refrigerated in an airtight container for up to 2 days, or freeze for up to 3 months.

Makes 1 dozen

chocolate orange cupcakes

see variations page 123

Orange extract helps sweeten the bitterness of the chocolate.

for the cupcakes
1 cup (2 sticks) sweet butter, softened
1 cup superfine sugar
2 cups self-rising flour
1 tsp. baking powder
4 eggs
1 tsp. orange extract

1 1/2 tbsp. grated orange zest
1/2 cup (3 1/2 oz.) semisweet chocolate chips

for the glaze
1/2 cup (3 1/2 oz.) semisweet chocolate chips
1/3 cup heavy cream
1 tsp. orange extract

Preheat the oven to 350°F (175°C). Place 18 paper baking cups into muffin pans. Combine all the cupcake ingredients, except the chocolate chips, in a large bowl and beat with an electric mixer until smooth and pale, about 2 to 3 minutes. Stir in the chocolate chips. Spoon the batter into the cups. Bake for 20 minutes. Remove pans from the oven and cool for 5 minutes. Then remove the cupcakes and cool on a rack.

For the chocolate glaze, melt the chocolate in a double boiler or medium bowl over a pan of simmering water, stirring until completely melted. Add the cream and orange extract, and stir until well combined. Cool slightly and pour over the cupcakes. Refrigerate until set.

Store unglazed in an airtight container for up to 2 days, or freeze for up to 3 months.

Makes 1 1/2 dozen

variations

chocolate mud cupcakes

see base recipe page 91

raspberry mud cupcakes
Prepare the basic cupcake recipe. Stir in 1/2 cup lightly crushed raspberries to the mixture after adding the melted chocolate.

white chocolate mud cupcakes
Prepare the basic cupcake recipe. Substitute 1 1/2 cups (10 1/2 oz.) white chocolate chips for the semisweet chocolate chips.

macadamia mud cupcakes
Prepare the basic cupcake recipe. Toast and chop 1/2 cup (3 1/2 oz.) macadamia nuts, and stir them in after adding the melted chocolate.

variations

chocolate ice cream cupcakes

see base recipe page 92

vanilla ice cream cupcakes
Prepare the basic cupcake recipe, substituting 1 cup vanilla ice cream for the chocolate ice cream.

chocolate chip & mint ice cream cupcakes
Prepare the basic cupcake recipe, substituting 1 cup mint chocolate chip ice cream for the chocolate ice cream.

caramel ice cream cupcakes
Prepare the basic cupcake recipe, substituting 1 cup caramel swirl ice cream for the chocolate ice cream.

variations

chocolate brownie cupcakes

see base recipe page 94

pecan brownie cupcakes
Prepare the basic cupcake recipe. Stir 1/2 cup (3 1/2 oz.) chopped pecans
into the mixture with the chocolate chips.

dalmatian brownie cupcakes
Prepare the basic cupcake recipe, substituting white chocolate chips for half
the quantity of semisweet chocolate chips.

chocolate fudge-frosted brownie cupcakes
Prepare the basic cupcake recipe. To make the frosting, combine 1/2 cup
(3 1/2 oz.) semisweet chocolate, 2 tablespoons milk, and 4 tablespoons
sweet butter in a medium saucepan and stir until the chocolate has
melted. Cool slightly and add the confectioners' sugar. Mix until smooth.

variations

white chocolate & strawberry cupcakes

see base recipe page 95

chocolate & black pepper cupcakes
Prepare the basic cupcake recipe, but replace the white chocolate chips with semisweet chocolate chips. Stir in 1 teaspoon freshly ground black pepper.

balsamic vinegar & strawberry cupcakes
Prepare the basic cupcake recipe, substituting 2 teaspoons sweet balsamic vinegar for the vanilla extract. Omit the white chocolate chips.

white chocolate & raspberry cupcakes
Prepare the basic cupcake recipe, using 1 cup fresh or thawed frozen raspberries instead of strawberries.

variations

chocolate & chili cupcakes

see base recipe page 96

white chocolate & chili cupcakes
Prepare the basic cupcake recipe, substituting white chocolate chips for the semisweet chocolate chips.

vodka-frosted chocolate & chili cupcakes
Prepare the basic cupcake recipe. For the frosting, substitute 3 tablespoons vodka for the Tia Maria.

orange liqueur-frosted chocolate & chili cupcakes
Prepare the basic cupcake recipe. For the frosting, substitute 3 tablespoons Grand Marnier or another orange liqueur for the Tia Maria.

white chocolate & macadamia nut cupcakes

see base recipe page 99

white chocolate & apricot cupcakes
Prepare the basic cupcake recipe, substituting 1/4 cup (2 oz.) finely
chopped dried apricots for half the white chocolate chips.

white chocolate & almond cupcakes
Prepare the basic cupcake recipe, substituting 1/4 cup (2 oz.) chopped
blanched almonds for half the white chocolate chips. For the frosting,
substitute 3 tablespoons toasted almonds for the macadamia nuts.

cranberry, orange, & macadamia nut cupcakes
Prepare the basic cupcake recipe, using only 1/4 cup (2 oz.) white
chocolate chips and adding 1/2 cup (3 1/2 oz.) dried cranberries and
1 tablespoon orange zest.

choc fudge-frosted cupcakes

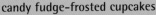

see base recipe page 100

candy fudge-frosted cupcakes
Prepare the basic cupcake recipe. For the frosting, add 1/2 cup (3 1/2 oz.) lightly crushed chocolate candies to the mixture after creaming the other ingredients.

white chocolate fudge-frosted cupcakes
Prepare the basic cupcake recipe. For the frosting, substitute 1/2 cup (3 1/2 oz.) white chocolate for the semisweet chocolate, and add 1 teaspoon vanilla extract.

fudge-frosted raisin cupcakes
Prepare the basic cupcake recipe, and add 1/2 cup (3 1/2 oz.) golden raisins to the mixture after creaming the batter.

variations

devil's food cupcakes

see base recipe page 101

coffee-frosted devil's cupcakes
Prepare the basic cupcake recipe. For the frosting, mix 1 teaspoon hot coffee with 2 tablespoons coffee granules and stir until dissolved. Leave to cool. Stir the cooled coffee into the chocolate frosting.

white chocolate-frosted devil's cupcakes
Prepare the basic cupcake recipe. For the frosting, substitute 1/2 cup (3 1/2 oz.) melted white chocolate for the semisweet chocolate.

hazelnut & chocolate-frosted devil's cupcakes
Prepare the basic cupcake recipe. For the frosting, add 1/2 cup (3 1/2 oz.) chopped toasted hazelnuts after combining the other ingredients.

choc 'n' cherry cupcakes

see base recipe page 103

slivered almond 'n' cherry cupcakes
Prepare the basic cupcake recipe, folding 3 tablespoons toasted slivered almonds to the cream after it has been whipped.

choc 'n' prune cupcakes
Prepare the basic cupcake recipe, substituting 1/2 cup (3 1/2 oz.) chopped prunes for the cherries. For the frosting, substitute 3 tablespoons chopped prunes for the whole cherries.

choc 'n' blueberry cupcakes
Prepare the basic cupcake recipe, substituting 1/2 cup (3 1/2 oz.) crushed blueberries for the cherries. For the frosting, substitute 3 tablespoons blueberries for the cherries.

variations

mint chocolate cupcakes

see base recipe page 104

raisin & mint chocolate cupcakes
Prepare the basic cupcake recipe, adding 1/2 cup (3 1/2 oz.) golden raisins along with the chocolate chips.

extra minty cupcakes
Prepare the basic cupcake recipe, substituting 1/2 cup (3 1/2 oz.) mint chocolate chips for the semisweet chocolate chips.

orange & mint cupcakes
Prepare the basic cupcake recipe, substituting 1/2 cup (3 1/2 oz.) orange chocolate chunks for the semisweet chocolate chips.

variations

chocolate chip & raisin brioches

see base recipe page 107

saffron, chocolate chip, & raisin brioches
Prepare the basic cupcake recipe, adding a pinch of saffron to the
dry ingredients.

white chocolate & macadamia nut brioches
Prepare the basic cupcake recipe, substituting 1/2 cup (3 1/2 oz.) white
chocolate chips and 1/2 cup (3 1/2 oz.) chopped macadamia nuts for the
chocolate chips and raisins.

chocolate & cinnamon brioches
Prepare the basic cupcake recipe, adding 2 teaspoons cinnamon to the flour.

variations

chocolate hazelnut cupcakes

see base recipe page 108

chocolate hazelnut & cranberry cupcakes

Prepare the basic cupcake recipe, adding 3 tablespoons chopped dried cranberries to the egg mixture.

chocolate hazelnut & orange cupcakes

Prepare the basic cupcake recipe, adding 2 tablespoons finely grated orange zest to the egg mixture.

chocolate macadamia nut cupcakes

Prepare the basic cupcake recipe, substituting 1/2 cup (3 1/2 oz.) roasted and chopped macadamia nuts for the hazelnuts.

variations

chocolate orange cupcakes

see base recipe page 110

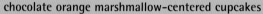

chocolate orange marshmallow-centered cupcakes

Bake and cool the cupcakes. Slice the top off each cupcake and hollow out
a small hole. Push 1 mini marshmallow into the hole. Place the "lid" back
on and frost with the chocolate glaze.

chocolate orange & vanilla custard cupcakes

Bake and cool the cupcakes. Slice the top off each cupcake and hollow out
a small hole. Pipe 1 teaspoon vanilla pie filling into the hole. Replace the
"lid" and frost with the chocolate glaze.

white chocolate & vanilla cupcakes

Prepare the basic cupcake recipe, substituting white chocolate chips for
the semisweet chocolate chips and vanilla extract for the orange extract.
Omit the orange zest. Use white chocolate chips for the glaze instead of
semisweet chocolate.

decadent cupcakes

The recipes in this chapter will leave no doubt in your mind that
the cupcake is most definitely a grown-up treat. From baked
cheesecakes to brioche bread pudding to Florentine cupcakes,
this chapter provides luxurious desserts in individual-size portions!

florentine cupcakes

see variations page 146

Savor *la dolce vita* when you bite into these Italian-inspired cupcakes.

for the cupcakes
1 cup (2 sticks) sweet butter, softened
1 cup superfine sugar
2 cups self-rising flour
4 eggs
1 tsp. vanilla extract

for the topping
3 tbsp. slivered almonds
3 tbsp. corn flakes
1/2 cup (3 1/2 oz.) roughly chopped candied
    cherries
3 tbsp. golden raisins
5 tbsp. condensed milk
2 oz. semisweet chocolate, melted
2 oz. white chocolate, melted

Preheat the oven to 350°F (175°C). Place 18 paper baking cups in muffin pans. Combine all the cupcake ingredients in a large bowl and beat with an electric mixer until smooth and pale, about 2 to 3 minutes. Spoon the batter into the cups. Bake for 20 minutes. Remove pans from the oven and cool for 5 minutes. Then remove the cupcakes and cool on a rack.

For the florentine topping, combine all the ingredients except the chocolate in a small bowl. Spoon small teaspoons of the mixture onto silicone-lined cookie sheets. Bake for 5 minutes, until golden. Remove from the oven and cool for 1 minute. Remove the florentines from the sheet and crumble. Scatter over the cooled cupcakes and drizzle with the chocolate. Store in an airtight container for up to 2 days, or freeze for up to 3 months.

Makes 1 1/2 dozen

strawberries 'n' cream cupcakes

see variations page 147

This recipe is great for lazy summer days when plump, sweet, and juicy strawberries are at the height of their season.

for the cupcakes
1 cup (2 sticks) sweet butter, softened
1 cup superfine sugar
2 cups self-rising flour
4 eggs
1 tsp. vanilla extract

for the topping
1 cup heavy cream
4 tbsp. confectioners' sugar, sifted
1 tsp. vanilla extract
4 cups sliced small strawberries
4 tbsp. strawberry jell-o
1 tbsp. water

Preheat the oven to 350°F (175°C). Place 18 paper baking cups in muffin pans. Combine all the cupcake ingredients in a medium bowl and beat with an electric mixer until smooth and pale, about 2 to 3 minutes.

Spoon the batter into the cups. Bake for 20 minutes. Remove pans from the oven and cool for 5 minutes. Then remove the cupcakes and cool on a rack. For the topping, whisk the cream, confectioners' sugar, and vanilla in a small bowl until soft peaks form. Spoon onto the cupcakes and arrange the strawberries on top. In a small saucepan heat the jell-o and water until melted. Brush the mixture on top of the strawberries. Chill until ready to serve.

Store in an airtight container in the refrigerator for up to 2 days.

Makes 1 1/2 dozen

baked cheesecakes

see variations page 148

These mouthwatering little cupcakes make stunning individual desserts. Make them ahead of time and all you'll have to do is pop them on a plate when your guests are ready.

1 cup (4 1/2 oz.) graham cracker crumbs
5 tbsp. sweet butter, melted
2 cups ricotta cheese
2 cups cream cheese, softened

2 tsp. vanilla extract
1 1/2 cups confectioners' sugar, sifted
3 eggs
1 1/2 cups fresh blueberries

Preheat the oven to 325°F (160°C). Place 12 paper baking cups in a muffin pan.

Put the cracker crumbs into a medium bowl and stir in the butter. Spoon tablespoons of the crumb mixture into the cups, pressing firmly into the bottom. Chill until set.

In a large bowl, beat the ricotta until smooth. Add the cream cheese, vanilla, and confectioners' sugar, blending until smooth. Slowly add the eggs, blending well. Spoon the mixture into the cups.

Bake for 25 minutes. Remove pan from oven and cool for 5 minutes. Then remove the cupcakes and cool on a rack. Chill until time to serve. Serve topped with blueberries.

Store covered for up to 2 days in the refrigerator.

Makes 1 dozen

kahlua & orange cupcakes

see variations page 149

The combination of Kahlua and orange is wonderful. It makes a delightful drink, and a scrumptious cupcake, too!

for the cupcakes
1 cup (2 sticks) sweet butter, softened
1 cup superfine sugar
2 cups self-rising flour
4 eggs
1 tsp. orange extract

for the frosting
2 cups confectioners' sugar, sifted
1/2 cup (1 stick) sweet butter, softened
1/4 cup sour cream
2 tbsp. Kahlua
1 tbsp. grated orange zest

Preheat the oven to 350°F (175°C). Place 18 paper baking cups in muffin pans. Combine all the cupcake ingredients in a medium bowl and beat with an electric mixer until smooth and pale, about 2 to 3 minutes. Spoon the batter into the cups. Bake for 20 minutes. Remove pans from the oven and cool for 5 minutes. Then remove the cupcakes and cool on a rack.

To make the frosting, beat the confectioners' sugar and butter in a small bowl until soft and creamy. Beat in the sour cream, Kahlua, and orange zest. Swirl onto the cooled cupcakes.

Store unfrosted in an airtight container for up to 2 days, or freeze for up to 3 months.

Makes 1 1/2 dozen

hot chocolate fondant cupcakes

see variations page 150

These cupcakes are very simple but must be served immediately. You can prepare the ramekins and batter in advance.

for the cupcakes
1 1/2 cups (7 1/2 oz.) bittersweet chocolate,
    broken into pieces
1 cup (2 sticks) sweet butter, softened
4 eggs
4 egg yolks
1/2 cup superfine sugar
3 tbsp. all-purpose flour

for the topping
1 cup sour cream
Cocoa powder or confectioners' sugar
    for dusting

Preheat the oven to 375°F (190°C). Butter 8 medium-sized ramekins. Dust each with flour, and tap out the excess. Melt the chocolate and butter in a double boiler or medium bowl over a pan of simmering water. Stir until smooth. Set aside to cool. In a large bowl, beat the eggs, egg yolks, and sugar until pale and creamy. Gradually add the melted chocolate, stirring until combined. Stir in the flour. Pour the batter into the prepared ramekins and bake for 15 minutes, or until the tops are set.

Turn out onto serving plates. Top each with a dollop of sour cream, and dust with cocoa powder or confectioners' sugar. Serve swiftly.

Makes 8

brioche bread pudding cupcakes

see variations page 151

Try this rich and robust cupcake recipe for an unusual and tasty twist on the classic bread pudding.

for the custard
2 eggs
1/2 cup superfine sugar
1 tsp. vanilla extract
2 cups heavy cream

for the cupcakes
12 thin slices brioche (crusts removed)
4 tbsp. sweet butter
3/4 cup fresh raspberries

To make the custard, cream the eggs, sugar, and vanilla in a small bowl. Add the cream, stir well, and put aside. Preheat the oven to 350°F (175°C). Grease 12 small molds with a little melted butter. Butter both sides of the bread and cut each slice into 12 small triangles. Push 3 triangles of bread into each mold, covering the bottom. Add a layer of raspberries. Pour a layer of custard over the raspberries. Repeat the process until there are four layers of each in each mold.

Place the molds in a roasting pan. Pour boiling water into the pan until it reaches half way up the molds. Bake until golden and firm, about 25 minutes. If the puddings begin to color too much, cover the pan with aluminum foil.

Turn the puddings out of the cups and serve warm. Store covered in the refrigerator for up to 2 days.

Makes 1 dozen

mini espresso cupcakes

see variations page 152

Making these cupcakes in espresso cups adds a special touch to the end of a meal.

for the cupcakes
1 1/2 cups all-purpose flour
1 1/2 tsp. baking powder
Pinch of salt
1/2 cup malted milk powder
1/4 cup dark espresso coffee
1 cup superfine sugar
2 eggs
1/2 cup (1 stick) sweet butter, softened

for the frosting
1 cup (2 sticks) sweet butter, softened
3 cups confectioners' sugar, sifted
1 tbsp. instant coffee granules
2 tsp. hot coffee
1 tsp. vanilla extract

Preheat the oven to 350°F (175°C). Place 18 paper baking cups in espresso cups or mini muffin pans. Sift the flour, baking powder, and salt into a medium bowl. Combine the milk powder and coffee in a small bowl. Beat the sugar, eggs, and butter in a medium bowl until light and creamy. Add the flour and coffee mixtures alternately to the egg mixture. Spoon the mixture into the cups. Bake for 15 minutes. Remove cups from oven and cool for 5 minutes. Then remove the cupcakes and cool on a rack.

To make the frosting, beat the butter and confectioners' sugar in a bowl until soft and creamy. Add the coffee granules to the hot coffee and stir. Beat into the butter and sugar mixture, and then stir in the vanilla. Spread the frosting onto the cooled cupcakes. Store unfrosted for up to 2 days in an airtight container, or freeze for up to 3 months.

Makes 1 1/2 dozen

almond & raspberry friands

see variations page 153

Try using different oval or rectangular-shaped friand pans. They are available from specialty cookware stores.

1 3/4 cups (2 sticks plus 3 tbsp.) sweet butter,
    softened
1 cup (3 1/2 oz.) ground almonds
6 egg whites

2/3 cup all-purpose flour
1/2 cup fresh raspberries
1/2 cup superfine sugar
Confectioners' sugar for dusting

Preheat the oven to 350°F (175°C). Grease 12 small friand pans with a little of the butter. Mix all the ingredients in a large bowl, reserving half the raspberries, until just combined.

Pour the batter into the prepared pans and scatter the remaining raspberries on top. Bake for 25 minutes, until golden and firm.

Remove pans from the oven and cool for 5 minutes. Turn friands out onto a rack and cool completely. Serve dusted with confectioners' sugar.

Store in an airtight container for up to 2 days.

Makes 1 dozen

key lime cupcakes

see variations page 154

An unusual take on the classic key lime pie. The cupcakes look great and taste even better!

for the cupcakes
1 cup (2 sticks) sweet butter, softened
1 cup superfine sugar
2 cups self-rising flour
4 eggs
1 tsp. vanilla extract

for the filling
1/3 cup key lime juice
14 oz. can condensed milk

for the meringue
3 egg whites
1/4 tsp. cream of tartar
1/3 cup granulated sugar

Preheat the oven to 350°F (175°C). Place 18 paper baking cups in muffin pans. Place all the cupcake ingredients in a large bowl, and beat with an electric mixer until smooth and pale, about 2 to 3 minutes. Spoon the batter into the cups. Bake for 20 minutes. Remove pans from the oven and cool for 5 minutes. Then remove the cupcakes and cool on a rack.

For the filling, combine the lime juice and condensed milk in a small bowl. Remove the top from each cupcake and hollow out a small hole. Spoon the filling into the hole and replace the top. For the meringue, beat the eggs and cream of tartar until soft peaks form. Add one-third of the sugar and beat for 1 minute. Repeat until all the sugar has been added. Increase the oven temperature to 450°F (230°C). Spoon or pipe the meringue on top of the cupcakes. Bake for 5 minutes until golden. Store for no more than 1 day in an airtight container.

Makes 1 1/2 dozen

mocha & walnut cupcakes

see variations page 155

The coffee and walnuts set off the sweetness of these delicious cupcakes.

for the cupcakes
1 cup (2 sticks) sweet butter, softened
1 cup superfine sugar
2 cups self-rising flour
4 eggs
1 tsp. vanilla extract
1/2 cup (3 1/2 oz.) chopped walnuts

for the frosting
1 cup (2 sticks) sweet butter, softened
3 cups confectioners' sugar, sifted
1 tbsp. instant coffee granules
1 tsp. hot coffee
1 tsp. coffee liqueur
1 tsp. vanilla extract

Preheat the oven to 350°F (175°C). Place 18 paper baking cups in muffin pans. Combine all the cupcake ingredients, except the walnuts, in a medium bowl and beat with an electric mixer until smooth and pale, about 2 to 3 minutes. Stir in the walnuts. Spoon the batter into the cups. Bake for 20 minutes. Remove pans from the oven and cool for 5 minutes. Then remove the cupcakes and cool on a rack.

For the frosting, beat the butter and confectioners' sugar in a bowl until soft and creamy. Combine the coffee granules and the hot coffee, then stir into the batter. Stir in the coffee liqueur and the vanilla. Spread the frosting onto the cooled cupcakes.

Store unfrosted for up to 2 days in an airtight container, or freeze for up to 3 months.

Makes 1 1/2 dozen

chocolate prune cupcakes

see variations page 156

The combination of bittersweet chocolate and prunes makes this cupcake pure decadence.

for the cupcakes
1 cup (2 sticks) sweet butter, softened
1 cup superfine sugar
2 cups self-rising flour
4 eggs
1 tsp. vanilla extract
1/2 cup (3 1/2 oz.) bittersweet chocolate chips
1/2 cup (3 1/2 oz.) chopped dried prunes

for the frosting
1 1/2 cups confectioners' sugar, sifted
1/2 cup (1 stick) sweet butter, softened
3/4 cup Dutch-process cocoa powder
2 tbsp. chocolate liqueur
1 tsp. vanilla extract

Preheat the oven to 350°F (175°C). Place 18 paper baking cups in muffin pans. Combine all the cupcake ingredients, except the chocolate chips and prunes, in a large bowl and beat with an electric mixer until smooth and pale, about 2 to 3 minutes. Stir in the prunes and chocolate. Spoon the batter into the cups. Bake in the oven for 20 minutes. Remove pans from the oven and cool for 5 minutes. Then remove the cupcakes and cool on a rack.

For the frosting, beat the confectioners' sugar and butter in a small bowl until creamy and smooth. Beat in the cocoa. Fold in the chocolate liqueur and vanilla. Spread the frosting onto the cooled cupcakes.

Store unfrosted in an airtight container for up to 3 days, or freeze for up to 3 months.

Makes 1 1/2 dozen

pineapple upside-down cupcakes

see variations page 157

A classic cake scaled down to a cupcake! When turning out the cupcakes, allow the sweet juices of the pineapple to be absorbed into the golden sponge.

for the topping
20 oz. can crushed pineapple
1/2 cup (1 stick) sweet butter, melted
3/4 cup packed brown sugar

for the cupcakes
1 cup (2 sticks) sweet butter, softened
1 cup superfine sugar
2 cups self-rising flour
4 eggs
1 tsp. vanilla extract

Preheat the oven to 350°F (175°C). Grease two 12-cup muffin pans with butter, and dust with a little flour, tapping out the excess. In the bottom of each cup, drizzle 1 tablespoon melted butter, 1 tablespoon pineapple, and 1 tablespoon brown sugar.

Place all the cupcake ingredients in a large bowl and beat with an electric mixer until smooth and pale, about 2 to 3 minutes. Spoon the batter on top of the pineapple mixture in each cup. Bake for 25 minutes. Remove pans from the oven and cool for 10 minutes.

Turn out the cupcakes onto dessert plates, serve warm with heavy cream if desired.

Store in an airtight container for up to 2 days.

Makes 2 dozen

little caramel cupcakes

see variations page 158

These delightful cupcakes contain a rich and gooey caramel surprise. They are an ideal companion for a cup of Earl Grey tea.

1/2 cup (1 stick) sweet butter, softened
3/4 cup packed brown sugar
2 lightly beaten eggs
2 tbsp. instant coffee granules

1 tbsp. boiling water
2 2/3 cups self-rising flour
1/2 cup milk
1/2 cup (3 1/2 oz.) soft caramels

Preheat the oven to 350°F (175°C). Place 12 paper baking cups in a muffin pan.

In a medium bowl, beat the butter and sugar until pale and creamy. Add the eggs slowly. In a small bowl, dissolve the coffee in the water. Beat the coffee into the butter mixture. Add the flour and milk, and beat until well combined.

Spoon the mixture into the cups. Push a couple of the caramels into the center of each cupcake, and place them in the oven.

Bake for 20 minutes. Cool for 5 minutes in the pan. Turn onto a plate and serve while warm.

Store in an airtight container for up to 2 days.

Makes 1 dozen

sticky toffee pudding cupcakes

see variations page 159

This is an old classic British pudding that has recently enjoyed a bit of a renaissance.

for the cupcakes
1 1/2 cups self-rising flour
2/3 cup packed brown sugar
1/2 cup milk
1 egg
1 tsp. vanilla extract
3 tbsp. sweet butter, melted
1 1/4 cups (7 oz.) chopped dates

for the topping
1/2 cup packed brown sugar
2 tbsp. sweet butter
2/3 cup boiling water

Preheat the oven to 375°F (190°C). Line 8 muffin pans with baking parchment. In a medium bowl, combine the flour and sugar. In a separate medium bowl beat the milk, eggs, vanilla, and butter until smooth and pale, about 2 to 3 minutes. Pour the batter over the flour mixture and stir with a wooden spoon. Fold in the dates. Scrape the mixture into the muffin pans, filling each cup about halfway. For the topping, sprinkle 1 tablespoon of the sugar on top of the batter in each cup. Add 1/2 tablespoon butter, then pour about 1 tablespoon water over each.

Bake for 25 minutes. Remove from oven and cool for 5 minutes in the pan. Invert onto plates, peel off the parchment, and serve immediately.

Makes 8

florentine cupcakes

see base recipe page 125

chocolate chip florentine cupcakes
Prepare the basic cupcake recipe, adding 1/2 cup (3 1/2 oz.) semisweet chocolate chips after creaming the batter.

cherry florentine cupcakes
Prepare the basic cupcake recipe, adding 3 tablespoons chopped candied cherries after creaming the batter.

almond florentine cupcakes
Prepare the basic cupcake recipe, adding 3 tablespoons chopped blanched almonds after creaming the batter.

strawberries 'n' cream cupcakes

see base recipe page 127

strawberries 'n' white chocolate cupcakes
Prepare the basic cupcake recipe, adding 1/2 cup (3 1/2 oz.) white chocolate chips to the creamed batter.

strawberries 'n' honey cupcakes
Prepare the basic cupcake recipe. For the topping, substitute 2 tablespoons honey for the confectioners' sugar.

strawberries 'n' lime cupcakes
Prepare the basic cupcake recipe. For the topping, substitute 1 tablespoon lime juice for the vanilla extract. Substitute 4 tablespoons lime jam for the strawberry jam.

variations

baked cheesecakes

see base recipe page 128

banana & raisin baked cheesecakes
Prepare the basic cupcake recipe, adding 1/2 cup mashed banana (about
1 banana) to the cheese mixture before adding the eggs. Add 4 tablespoons
raisins to the mixture after adding the eggs.

raspberry baked cheesecakes
Prepare the basic cupcake recipe, adding 1/2 cup fresh raspberries after
mixing in the egg.

maple syrup baked cheesecakes
Prepare the basic cupcake recipe, substituting 1/4 cup maple syrup for
the confectioners' sugar.

variations

kahlua & orange cupcakes

see base recipe page 130

white chocolate chip kahlua cupcakes
Prepare the basic cupcake recipe, adding 1/2 cup (3 1/2 oz.) white chocolate chips to the creamed batter.

semisweet chocolate chip kahlua cupcakes
Prepare the basic cupcake recipe, adding 1/2 cup (3 1/2 oz.) semisweet chocolate chips to the creamed batter.

raisin & brazil nut kahlua cupcakes
Prepare the basic cupcake recipe, adding 1/4 cup (2 oz.) raisins and 1/4 cup (2 oz.) chopped Brazil nuts to the creamed batter.

variations

hot chocolate fondant cupcakes

see base recipe page 131

strawberry cream fondant cupcakes
Prepare the basic cupcake recipe. Purée 5 medium-size, fresh strawberries in a food processor. Beat 1 cup heavy cream with 1 teaspoon vanilla extract until it is soft but holds its shape. Fold in the puréed strawberries. Spoon over the hot cupcakes.

orange cream fondant cupcakes
Prepare the basic cupcake recipe. Beat 1 cup heavy cream with 1 teaspoon orange extract and 2 tablespoons confectioners' sugar until it is soft but holds its shape. Spoon liberally over the hot cupcakes.

crème chantilly fondant cupakes
Prepare the basic cupcake recipe. Beat 1 cup heavy cream with 1 teaspoon vanilla extract and 2 tablespoons confectioners' sugar until it is soft but holds its shape. Spoon over the hot cupcakes.

variations

brioche bread pudding cupcakes

see base recipe page 132

blueberry bread pudding cupcakes
Prepare the basic cupcake recipe, substituting 3/4 cup fresh blueberries for the raspberries.

cherry bread pudding cupcakes
Prepare the basic cupcake recipe, substituting 3/4 cup (5 oz.) chopped candied cherries for the raspberries.

chocolate chip bread pudding cupcakes
Prepare the basic cupcake recipe, substituting 3/4 cup (5 oz.) semisweet chocolate chips for the raspberries.

variations

mini espresso cupcakes

see base recipe page 134

mini chocolate espresso cupcakes
Prepare the basic cupcake recipe, adding 3 tablespoons chocolate chips after creaming the batter.

mini cinnamon espresso cupcakes
Prepare the basic cupcake recipe, sifting 2 teaspoons cinnamon into the dry ingredients.

mini espresso cupcakes with Tia Maria
Prepare the basic cupcake recipe, adding 2 tablespoons Tia Maria liqueur to the frosting.

almond & raspberry friands

see base recipe page 135

strawberry friands
Prepare the basic cupcake recipe, substituting 1/2 cup fresh strawberries
for the raspberries.

chocolate & pecan friands
Prepare the basic cupcake recipe, substituting 3 tablespoons chopped pecans
and 3 tablespoons semisweet chocolate chips for the raspberries.

raisin friands
Prepare the basic cupcake recipe, substituting 1/2 cup (3 1/2 oz.) raisins for
the raspberries.

variations

key lime cupcakes

see base recipe page 136

ice cream meringue cupcakes
Prepare the basic cupcake recipe, substituting 1 teaspoon ice cream for the
original filling. Pop the cupcakes in the freezer until ready to serve.

chocolate meringue cupcakes
Prepare the basic cupcake recipe. For the filling, substitute 1/2 cup (3 1/2 oz.)
semisweet chocolate chips for the milk and lime juice. Melt the chocolate
in a double boiler and cool slightly. Spoon the chocolate into the hole and
refrigerate until set. Decorate with the meringue when the chocolate has
cooled. Bake for 5 minutes until meringue is golden.

lemon meringue cupcakes
Prepare the basic cupcake recipe. For the filling, substitute 1/3 cup lemon
juice for the key lime juice.

mocha & walnut cupcakes

see base recipe page 138

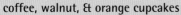

coffee, walnut, & orange cupcakes
Prepare the basic cupcake recipe. For the frosting, substitute 1 tablespoon grated orange zest for the vanilla extract.

irish cream & walnut cupcakes
Prepare the basic cupcake recipe. For the frosting, substitute 2 tablespoons Irish Cream liqueur for the vanilla extract and coffee liqueur.

chocolate chip & walnut cupcakes
Prepare the basic cupcake recipe, adding 1/4 cup (2 oz.) semisweet chocolate chips after creaming the cupcake batter.

chocolate prune cupcakes

see base recipe page 139

orange, chocolate, & prune cupcakes

Prepare the basic cupcake recipe, adding 1 tablespoon finely grated orange zest to the creamed batter.

walnut, chocolate, & prune cupcakes

Prepare the basic cupcake recipe, adding 1/4 cup (2 oz.) chopped walnuts after mixing in the chocolate chips and prunes.

hazelnut, chocolate, & prune cupcakes

Prepare the basic cupcake recipe, adding 1/4 cup (2 oz.) chopped toasted hazelnuts after mixing in the chocolate chips and prunes.

variations

pineapple upside-down cupcakes

see base recipe page 140

cherry pineapple upside-down cupcakes
Prepare the basic cupcake recipe. Add 1/2 cup (3 1/2 oz.) chopped cherries
to the pineapple mixture.

almond pineapple upside-down cupcakes
Prepare the basic cupcake recipe, adding 3 tablespoons chopped blanched
almonds to the creamed batter.

orange pineapple upside-down cupcakes
Prepare the basic cupcake recipe, adding 2 teaspoons orange extract to the
cupcake batter.

variations

little caramel cupcakes

see base recipe page 143

chocolate chip & caramel cupcakes
Prepare the basic cupcake recipe, mixing 4 tablespoons semisweet chocolate chips into the batter after the milk has been added.

ginger & caramel cupcakes
Prepare the basic cupcake recipe, mixing 3 tablespoons chopped candied ginger into the batter after the milk has been added.

chocolate nougat cupcakes
Prepare the basic cupcake recipe, substituting 6 1/2 mini Baby Ruth bars for the caramel.

sticky toffee pudding cupcakes

see base recipe page 144

date & apricot pudding cupcakes
Prepare the basic cupcake recipe. Substitute 2/3 cup (4 oz.) dried apricots for half the chopped dates.

date & walnut pudding cupcakes
Prepare the basic cupcake recipe. Substitute 2/3 cup (4 oz.) chopped walnuts for half the chopped dates.

date & pistachio pudding cupcakes
Prepare the basic cupcake recipe. Substitute 2/3 cup (4 oz.) chopped pistachios for half the chopped dates.

muffins

Muffins are hearty, homey, and delicious. They can be served
at any time of day — breakfast, brunch or lunch, tea or dinner.
Muffins generally have fuller tops than cupcakes and are most
likely to be served without any type of frosting or topping.

blueberry muffins

see variations page 179

These classics are a great way to start the day. Serve them warm from the oven with a steaming cup of coffee or tea. If you can't get fresh blueberries, use frozen.

1/2 cup superfine sugar
1 tbsp. grated lemon zest
2 1/2 cups all-purpose flour
1 tbsp. baking powder
2 lightly beaten eggs

1 cup milk
1/2 cup (1 stick) sweet butter, melted
1 tsp. vanilla extract
2 cups fresh or thawed frozen blueberries

Preheat the oven to 400°F (200°C). Place 12 paper baking cups in a muffin pan.

In a medium bowl, stir the sugar, lemon zest, flour, and baking powder with a spoon. In a large bowl, beat the eggs, milk, butter, and vanilla with an electric mixer until smooth, about 1 minute. Add the dry ingredients and stir until the blueberries are just combined. Spoon the batter into the cups.

Bake in the oven for 20 minutes. Remove pan from the oven and cool for 5 minutes. Serve muffins immediately.

Store in an airtight container for up to 2 days, or freeze for up to 3 months.

Makes 1 dozen

raspberry & coffee muffins

see variations page 180

The combination of fruit and nuts gives these muffins a wonderful texture.

2 tbsp. boiling water
2 tbsp. instant coffee granules
1 tbsp. milk
1/2 cup (1 stick) sweet butter, melted
3 tbsp. chopped hazelnuts
3 1/2 cups self-rising flour

1 1/3 cups superfine sugar
1 tsp. baking soda
2 lightly beaten eggs
1 1/2 cups buttermilk
1 cup fresh raspberries

Preheat the oven to 400°F (200°C). Grease a 12-cup muffin pan. In a cup or small bowl, pour 2 tablespoons boiling water over the instant coffee. Stir in the milk. Set aside to cool. In a medium bowl, mix the hazelnuts, flour, sugar, and baking soda with a spoon.

In a large bowl, beat the eggs and buttermilk with an electric mixer until combined, about 2 to 3 minutes. Stir in the cooled coffee. Add the flour mixture to the buttermilk mixture, stirring until nearly combined. Gently fold in the raspberries. Spoon the batter into the prepared pan.

Bake for 20 minutes. Remove pan from the oven and cool for 5 minutes. Serve immediately.

Store in an airtight container for up to 2 days, or freeze for up to 3 months.

Makes 1 dozen

beet & chocolate muffins

see variations page 181

Do not be alarmed — these muffins are truly marvelous! Use fresh beets, with the skin on, not canned.

1 1/2 lb. (about 2 large) fresh trimmed beets
3 1/2 cups self-rising flour
2 tbsp. Dutch-process cocoa powder
1 cup superfine sugar

1 tsp. baking powder
2 eggs
1/2 cup vegetable oil
1 1/2 cups buttermilk

Steam the beets for 50 minutes, until tender. Drain and rinse under cold water. When cool enough to handle, gently peel away the skin with your fingertips. You may need to wear latex gloves to avoid staining your hands purple. Place the peeled beets in a food processor and blend until smooth. Set aside.

Preheat the oven to 350°F (175°C). Grease a 12-cup muffin pan. In a medium bowl, combine the flour, cocoa, sugar, and baking powder. In a large bowl, beat the eggs, oil, and buttermilk. Stir in the beets until well combined. Add the flour mixture, stirring until just combined.

Spoon the batter in the prepared pan. Bake for 20 minutes. Remove pan from the oven and cool for 5 minutes. Then remove the muffins and cool on a rack.

Store in an airtight container for up to 2 days, or freeze for up to 3 months.

Makes 1 dozen

tomato & basil muffins

see variations page 182

Tomato and basil are a classic combination. Treat your basil kindly, and don't chop it too much.

2 tbsp. chopped fresh basil
2 3/4 cups all-purpose flour
2 tbsp. baking powder
Pinch of salt

4 lightly beaten eggs
1/2 cup olive oil
10 3/4 oz. can condensed tomato soup
3 tbsp. sun-dried tomatoes

Preheat the oven to 350°F (175°C). Grease a 12-cup muffin pan.

In a medium bowl, mix the basil, flour, baking powder, and salt with a spoon.

In a large bowl, combine the eggs, olive oil, soup, and sun-dried tomatoes with an electric mixer until well combined. Mix the flour mixture into the soup mixture until just combined.

Spoon the mixture into the prepared pan. Bake for 20 minutes. Remove pan from the oven and cool for 5 minutes. Remove the muffins and cool on a rack. Serve warm.

Store in an airtight container for up to 3 days, or freeze for up to 3 months.

Makes 1 dozen

apple & cinnamon muffins

see variations page 183

The apple and cinnamon complement each other without competing for attention.

2 3/4 cups all-purpose flour
1 1/4 cups superfine sugar
4 tsp. baking powder
2 tsp. cinnamon
4 tbsp. vegetable oil

1/4 cup sweet butter, melted
2 lightly beaten eggs
3/4 cup buttermilk
2 small apples, peeled, cored, and finely diced

Preheat the oven to 350°F (175°C). Grease a 12-cup muffin pan.

In a medium bowl, combine the flour, sugar, baking powder, and cinnamon. Set aside.

In a large bowl, beat the oil, butter, eggs, and buttermilk with an electric mixer until well combined. Add the flour mixture and beat until nearly combined. Stir in the apples. Do not overmix. Spoon the mixture into the prepared pan.

Bake for 20 minutes. Remove pan from the oven and cool for 5 minutes. Then remove the muffins and cool on a rack.

Store in an airtight container for up to 2 days, or freeze for up to 3 months.

Makes 1/2 dozen

corn muffins

see variations page 184

These splendid little muffins lend themselves to all manner of occasions. They work well with hearty dishes like chili and pot roast.

2 1/4 cups self-rising flour
1 1/2 cups cornmeal
1/2 cup superfine sugar
1 tsp. baking powder
Pinch of salt

1 cup buttermilk
3/4 cup sweet butter, melted
1 lightly beaten egg

Preheat the oven to 350°F (175°C). Grease a large 6-cup muffin pan.

In a medium bowl, mix the flours, cornmeal, sugar, baking powder, and salt with a spoon. Beat the buttermilk, butter, and egg in a large bowl with an electric mixer. Stir the dry ingredients into the buttermilk mixture until just combined.

Spoon the batter into the prepared pan. Bake for 20 minutes. Remove pan from the oven and cool for 5 minutes. Remove the muffins and cool on a rack. Serve warm.

Store in an airtight container for up to 2 days, or freeze for up to 3 months.

Makes 1/2 dozen

mixed berry crumble muffins

see variations page 185

These crumbly-topped muffins hide a sweet surprise. Serve them right out of the oven!

for the filling
2 1/2 cups mixed berries (blackberries,
    strawberries, raspberries)
3 tbsp. superfine sugar
2 tbsp. water
1/4 tsp. lemon zest

for the crumble
2 tbsp. sweet butter, melted
4 tbsp. all-purpose flour
3 tbsp. light brown sugar

4 tbsp. rolled oats
1 tsp. lemon zest

for the muffins
3 cups self-rising flour
3/4 cup packed brown sugar
Pinch of salt
1 tsp. baking powder
1/2 cup (1 stick) sweet butter, melted
1 1/4 cups milk
1 egg

Preheat the oven to 400°F (200°C). Grease a 12-cup muffin pan. Combine all the filling ingredients in a small saucepan. Gently bring to a simmer, and cook for 5 minutes, until the berries give some of their juices. Set aside. Stir all the crumble ingredients in a small bowl and set aside. For the muffins, combine the dry ingredients in a large bowl. In a medium bowl, beat the butter, milk, and egg. Add the egg mixture to the dry ingredients and stir until just combined. Using about half the batter, spoon a little batter into each cup, then spoon a layer of the filling. Add the remaining batter, and top with the crumble mixture. Bake for 20 minutes. Remove pan from the oven and cool for 5 minutes. Serve muffins warm. Store in an airtight container for up to 3 days, or freeze for up to 3 months.

Makes 1 dozen

rhubarb & pistachio muffins

see variations page 186

The pistachios and rhubarb give these muffins a wonderful color.

for the filling
1 1/4 cups chopped fresh rhubarb
4 tbsp. superfine sugar
2 tbsp. water
1 tsp. grated lemon zest

for the muffins
3 1/2 cups all-purpose flour
2/3 cup packed brown sugar
Pinch of salt
4 tsp. baking powder
1/2 cup (1 stick) sweet butter, melted
1 1/4 cups milk
1 lightly beaten egg
1/2 cup shelled pistachios

Preheat the oven to 400°F (200°C). Grease a 12-cup muffin pan. Combine all the filling ingredients in a saucepan over gentle heat. Bring slowly to a simmer and cook for 5 minutes, until the rhubarb is soft. Set aside. In a medium bowl, combine the flour, sugar, salt, and baking powder. Mix well and set aside. In a large bowl, combine the butter, milk, and egg with an electric mixer until combined. Stir in the flour mixture until nearly combined, then stir in the pistachios. Spoon a little mixture into the muffin cups, top with the cooled rhubarb, and finally add the remaining muffin mixture. Bake for 20 minutes. Remove from the oven and cool for 5 minutes. Then remove the muffins and cool on a rack.

Store in an airtight container for up to 2 days, or freeze for up to 3 months.

Makes 1 dozen

peach & tomato muffins

see variations page 187

The marriage of peach and tomato may be unusual, but these muffins taste fantastic!

3 1/2 cups self-rising flour
1 tsp. baking powder
Pinch of salt
4 tbsp. superfine sugar
1/3 cup (2/3 stick) sweet butter, melted

1 lightly beaten egg
1 1/3 cups buttermilk
2 ripe medium peaches, sliced
3 tbsp. chopped sun-dried tomatoes

Preheat the oven to 400°F (200°C). Grease a large 6-cup muffin pan.

In a medium bowl, mix the flour, baking powder, salt, and sugar with a spoon.

In a large bowl, beat the butter, egg, and buttermilk with an electric mixer. Add the flour to the buttermilk mixture, stirring until nearly combined. Stir in the peaches and tomatoes.

Spoon the batter into the prepared pan. Bake for 20 minutes. Remove pan from the oven and cool for 5 minutes. Remove the muffins and cool on a rack.

Store refrigerated in an airtight container for up to 2 days, or freeze for up to 3 months.

Makes 1/2 dozen

smoked salmon &
cracked pepper muffins

see variartions page 188

This muffin goes with any meal. Try serving it for brunch, slightly warm, with a soft-boiled egg.

2 cups all-purpose flour
1 tbsp. baking powder
Pinch of salt
1 cup milk
2 lightly beaten eggs

3 tbsp. sweet butter, melted
3 1/2 oz. finely chopped smoked salmon
1 tsp. freshly ground black pepper
1 tbsp. grated lemon zest

Preheat the oven to 350°F (175°C). Grease a large 6-cup muffin pan.

In a medium bowl, combine the flour, baking powder, and salt with a spoon.

In a large bowl, beat the milk, eggs, and butter with an electric mixer. Add the salmon, black pepper, and lemon zest. Gently fold the flour into the wet ingredients until just combined.

Spoon the mixture into the prepared pan. Bake for 20 minutes. Remove from the oven and cool for 5 minutes. Then remove the muffins and cool on a rack.

Store refrigerated in an airtight container for up to 2 days, or freeze for up to 3 months.

Makes 1/2 dozen

morning granola muffins

see variations page 189

If you are usually in a hurry to get out the door in the morning, make a batch of these delicious and nutritious muffins the night before.

1 cup (6 oz.) finely chopped dried apricots
1 1/4 cups dried granola
2 1/4 cups self-rising flour
1 tsp. baking powder
1/2 cup orange juice

1/2 cup apple juice
3 tbsp. vegetable oil
3/4 cup honey
1 lightly beaten egg

Preheat the oven to 350°F (175°C). Grease a 12-cup muffin pan.

Mix the apricots, granola, flour, and baking powder in a medium bowl with a spoon. Set aside. Beat the orange juice, apple juice, oil, honey, and egg in a large bowl with an electric mixer. Add the flour mixture to the egg mixture, and stir until just combined.

Spoon the mixture into the prepared pan. Bake for 20 minutes. Remove pan from the oven and cool for 5 minutes. Then remove the muffins and cool on a rack.

Store in an airtight container for up to 3 days, or freeze for up to 3 months.

Makes 1 dozen

caramelized onion muffins

see variations page 190

You can use any kind of onion in this recipe. You could try Vidalia onions, which have an incredible natural sweetness.

2 tbsp. olive oil
1 lb. (about 3) finely sliced medium
    Vidalia onions
1 tsp. dried crushed chilies
4 cups all-purpose flour
2 1/4 cups cornmeal

1 tbsp. baking powder
Pinch of salt
2 lightly beaten eggs
1 1/2 cups sweet butter, melted
1 1/3 cups buttermilk
1 tbsp. chopped fresh thyme leaves

Heat the oil in a medium skillet. Add the onions and cook over medium heat, stirring occasionally until they are soft and caramelized, about 15 minutes. Set aside to cool.

Preheat the oven to 350°F (175°C). Grease a 12-cup muffin pan.

In a medium bowl, mix the chilies, flour, cornmeal, baking powder, and salt with a spoon. In a large bowl, beat the eggs, butter, buttermilk, and thyme until combined. Stir in half the cooked onions. Stir in the flour mixture until just combined. Spoon the mixture into the prepared pan. Top with the remaining cooked onions. Bake for 20 minutes. Remove pan from the oven and cool for 5 minutes. Then remove the muffins and serve warm.

Store in an airtight container for up to 2 days. Not suitable for freezing.

Makes 1 dozen

white chocolate &
macadamia nut muffins

see variations page 191

There can't be a more decadent combination than white chocolate and macadamia nuts!

2 cups self-rising flour
1/2 cup superfine sugar
1 cup (7 oz.) white chocolate chips
1/2 cup roughly chopped, lightly toasted
   macadamia nuts

Pinch of salt
4 tbsp. butter, melted
3/4 cup buttermilk
1 lightly beaten egg

Preheat the oven to 350°F (175°C). Grease a large 6-cup muffin pan.

In a medium bowl, mix the flour, sugar, chocolate chips, nuts, and salt with a spoon.

In a large bowl, beat the butter, buttermilk, and egg with an electric mixer. Add the flour mixture to the buttermilk mixture, stirring until just combined. Do not overmix.

Spoon the mixture into the prepared pan. Bake for 25 minutes. Remove pan from the oven and cool for 5 minutes. Then remove the muffins and cool on a rack.

Store in an airtight container for up to 3 days, or freeze for up to 3 months.

Makes 1/2 dozen

variations

blueberry muffins

see base recipe page 161

strawberry muffins
Prepare the basic cupcake recipe, substituting 2 cups quartered fresh strawberries for the blueberries.

raspberry muffins
Prepare the basic cupcake recipe, substituting 2 cups fresh raspberries for the blueberries.

blackberry muffins
Prepare the basic cupcake recipe, substituting 2 cups halved fresh blackberries for the blueberries.

variations

raspberry & coffee muffins

see base recipe page 163

raspberry & pine nut muffins
Prepare the basic muffin recipe, substituting 3 tablespoons whole pine nuts for the hazelnuts.

blueberry & coffee muffins
Prepare the basic muffin recipe, substituting 1 cup fresh blueberries for the raspberries.

mixed berry & coffee muffins
Prepare the basic muffin recipe, substituting 1/2 cup fresh blackberries for half the raspberries.

variations

beet & chocolate muffins

see base recipe page 164

beet, chocolate, & orange muffins
Prepare the basic muffin recipe, adding 1 teaspoon orange extract to
the batter before stirring in the beets.

beet & chocolate chip muffins
Prepare the basic muffin recipe, adding 3 tablespoons semisweet chocolate
chips to the dry ingredients.

beet, chocolate, & fennel muffins
Prepare the basic muffin recipe, adding 1 tablespoon crushed fennel seeds
to the dry ingredients.

variations

tomato & basil muffins

see base recipe page 165

tomato, basil, & mozzarella muffins
Prepare the basic muffin recipe, adding 1/2 cup (3 1/2 oz.) shredded mozzarella cheese to the soup mixture.

tomato & marjoram muffins
Prepare the basic muffin recipe, substituting 2 tablespoons chopped fresh marjoram for the basil.

tomato & chive muffins
Prepare the basic muffin recipe, substituting 2 tablespoons chopped fresh chives for the basil.

apple & cinnamon muffins

see base recipe page 167

apple, cinnamon, & walnut muffins
Prepare the basic muffin recipe, adding 1/2 cup (3 1/2 oz.) chopped walnuts along with the apples.

pear & cinnamon muffins
Prepare the basic muffin recipe, substituting 2 medium-sized pears for the apples.

apple & spice muffins
Prepare the basic muffin recipe, adding 1/2 teaspoon ground cloves to the dry ingredients.

variations

corn muffins

see base recipe page 168

chili & cilantro corn muffins

Prepare the basic muffin recipe, adding 1 teaspoon seeded and finely
chopped red chili pepper and 3 tablespoons freshly chopped cilantro
to the dry ingredients.

holy trinity corn muffins

Prepare the basic muffin recipe, adding 3 tablespoons finely diced red
pepper, 2 tablespoons finely diced green pepper, and 2 tablespoons finely
chopped basil to the dry ingredients.

spicy sausage corn muffins

Prepare the basic muffin recipe, adding 1/2 cup (3 1/2 oz.) cooked
chopped Italian-style sausage.

variations

mixed berry crumble muffins

see base recipe page 169

apple crumble muffins
Prepare the basic muffin recipe, substituting 1 1/2 cups unsweetened applesauce for the mixed berries.

peach crumble muffins
Prepare the basic muffin recipe, substituting 1 1/2 cups canned sliced peaches for the mixed berries.

rhubarb crumble muffins
Prepare the basic muffin recipe, substituting 1 1/2 cups drained cooked rhubarb for the mixed berries.

variations

rhubarb & pistachio muffins

see base recipe page 171

rhubarb & ginger muffins
Prepare the basic muffin recipe, substituting 3 tablespoons chopped candied ginger for the pistachios.

rhubarb & custard muffins
Prepare the basic muffin recipe. When the muffins have cooled, slice the top off each. Using a teaspoon, scoop out a small hole and fill with 1 teaspoon prepared custard (or vanilla pie filling). Replace the "lid" of the cupcake.

rhubarb & orange flower muffins
Prepare the basic muffin recipe, adding 2 tablespoons orange flower water to the butter mixture.

variations

peach & tomato muffins

see base recipe page 172

peach, tomato, & lime muffins
Prepare the basic muffin recipe, adding 1 tablespoon freshly grated
lime zest to the buttermilk mixture.

peach, tomato, & basil muffins
Prepare the basic muffin recipe, adding 2 tablespoons freshly chopped
basil to the buttermilk mixture.

peach, tomato, & rosemary muffins
Prepare the basic muffin recipe, adding 1 teaspoon freshly chopped
rosemary to the buttermilk mixture.

smoked salmon & cracked pepper muffins

see base recipe page 174

smoked salmon & asparagus muffins

Prepare the basic muffin recipe, adding 1 cup cooked chopped asparagus to the batter along with the salmon.

smoked salmon & mustard muffins

Prepare the basic muffin recipe, adding 2 tablespoons whole-grain mustard to the muffin batter along with the salmon.

smoked salmon & egg muffins

Prepare the basic muffin recipe. Place a whole soft-boiled egg in each muffin cup. Pour the muffin batter around and over it.

morning granola muffins

see base recipe page 175

peach granola muffins
Prepare the basic muffin recipe, substituting 1 cup (7 oz.) dried peaches for the apricots.

coconut granola muffins
Prepare the basic muffin recipe, adding 4 tablespoons dried flaked coconut to the dried ingredients.

maple granola muffins
Prepare the basic muffin recipe, substituting 3/4 cup maple syrup for the honey.

variations

caramelized onion muffins

see base recipe page 176

onion & rosemary muffins

Prepare the basic muffin recipe, substituting 1 tablespoon fresh rosemary for the thyme.

onion & gruyère muffins

Prepare the basic muffin recipe, adding 1 cup (4 oz.) shredded Gruyère cheese to the batter before adding the onions.

two onion muffins

Prepare the basic muffin recipe, adding 3 tablespoons finely sliced green onions along with the other onions.

white chocolate & macadamia nut muffins

see base recipe page 178

white chocolate & date-nut muffins
Prepare the basic muffin recipe, adding 3 tablespoons chopped
dates to the mixture.

white chocolate & vanilla muffins
Prepare the basic muffin recipe, adding 1 teaspoon vanilla extract
to the buttermilk mixture.

white chocolate & pecan muffins
Prepare the basic muffin recipe, substituting 1/2 cup (3 1/2 oz.)
chopped pecan nuts for the macadamia nuts.

cupcakes for special occasions

This chapter will provide inspiration for your next special occasion,

whether a holiday like Valentine's Day, or a birthday or wedding.

st. patrick's day muffins

see variations page 212

These muffins are ideal to line the stomach before embarking on a day of toasting the Irish. Yes, they contain potatoes!

2 medium potatoes, peeled and cut into
    1/2 in. (6 mm) cubes
2 3/4 cups all-purpose flour
Pinch of salt
1 tbsp. baking powder

1 lightly beaten egg
4 tbsp. vegetable oil
1 1/4 cups buttermilk
3 tbsp. chopped fresh chives
3 tbsp. chopped fresh parsley

Preheat the oven to 350°F (175°C). Grease a 12-cup muffin pan with a little oil. In a small saucepan, cook the potatoes in boiling salted water for 8 minutes, or until just tender. Drain and rinse under cold water and set aside. In a medium bowl, combine the flour, salt, and baking powder. In a large bowl, beat the egg, oil, buttermilk, chives, and parsley. Stir the flour mixture into the buttermilk mixture until nearly combined. Gently fold in the potatoes.

Spoon the mixture into the prepared pan. Bake for 20 minutes.

Remove pan from the oven and cool for 5 minutes. Then remove the muffins and cool on a rack. Serve with a glass of Guinness!

Store in an airtight container for up to 2 days, or freeze for up to 3 months.

Makes 1 dozen

easter egg nests

see variations page 213

These cute nests make the perfect gift for your little Easter bunnies.

for the cupcakes
1 cup (2 sticks) sweet butter, softened
1 cup superfine sugar
2 cups self-rising flour
4 eggs
1 tsp. vanilla extract

for the frosting
10 oz. chocolate, flaked
2 tbsp. heavy cream
3/4 cup (4 1/2 oz.) semisweet chocolate,
    chopped
54 candy-covered mini chocolate eggs

Preheat the oven to 350°F (175°C). Place 18 paper baking cups in muffin pans. Combine all the cupcake ingredients in a large bowl and beat with an electric mixer until smooth and pale, about 2 to 3 minutes. Spoon the batter into the cups.

Bake for 20 minutes. Remove pans from the oven and cool for 5 minutes. Then remove the cupcakes and cool on a rack.

To make the frosting, put the chocolate and cream in a small saucepan over a low heat. Stir gently until combined. Remove from the heat and stir until the mixture is smooth. Swirl onto the cooled cupcakes. Top with shards of the chocolate and place 3 mini eggs on top.

Store unfrosted in an airtight container for up to 3 days, or freeze for up to 3 months.

Makes 1 1/2 dozen

wedding cupcakes

see variations page 214

These cupcakes are perfect for a home-style wedding. Each of your guests can take one home as a memento of the day.

for the cupcakes
1 cup (2 sticks) sweet butter, softened
1 cup superfine sugar
2 cups self-rising flour
4 eggs
1 tsp. vanilla extract

for the frosting
1/2 cup confectioners' sugar
2 tbsp. lemon juice
54 candy-coated almonds
18 frosted roses

Preheat the oven to 350°F (175°C). Place 18 paper baking cups in muffin pans. Combine all the cupcake ingredients in a large bowl and beat with an electric mixer until smooth and pale, about 2 to 3 minutes.

Spoon the batter into the cups. Bake for 20 minutes. Remove pans from the oven and cool for 5 minutes. Then remove the cupcakes and cool on a rack.

To make the frosting, sift the confectioners' sugar into a medium bowl. Add the lemon juice gradually, until it holds its shape. Spread onto the cupcakes, and top with almonds and roses.

Store unfrosted in an airtight container for up to 3 days, or freeze for up to 3 months.

Makes 1 1/2 dozen

halloween pumpkin muffins

see variations page 215

Decorate these cupcakes with skeletons for when the trick-or-treaters come calling.

for the muffins
1 1/2 cups all-purpose flour
1 tsp. cinnamon
1 tsp. baking soda
1 tsp. baking powder
1 tsp. allspice
1 1/4 cups superfine sugar
1/2 cup vegetable oil

2 lightly beaten eggs
1/2 cup milk
1 cup pumpkin purée

for the frosting
2 oz. orange ready-rolled fondant frosting
2 oz. black ready-rolled fondant frosting
3 tbsp. strawberry jam

Preheat the oven to 350°F (175°C). Place 6 large paper baking cups in a muffin pan.

Dust two cookie sheets with confectioners' sugar. In a medium bowl, mix the dry ingredients. In a large bowl, beat the oil, eggs, and milk. Stir in the pumpkin purée. Combine the flour mixture into the pumpkin mixture, and spoon into the cups. Bake for 20 minutes. Remove pan and cool for 5 minutes. Then remove the muffins and cool on a rack. For the frosting, roll the orange fondant to 1/8 in. (3 mm) thick. Use a cutter or stencil to cut out Halloween shapes. Lay on one of the cookie sheets. Roll the black fondant to 1/8 in. (3 mm) thick. Cut 6 circles about 2 1/2 in. (6 cm) across. Set on the other cookie sheet. Brush the top of each muffin with some jam. Lay the black fondant circles on top, followed by the Halloween shapes. Sprinkle with candies. Store in an airtight container for up to 2 days.

Makes 1/2 dozen

passover cupcakes

see variations page 216

Make these with matzoh meal, also known as cake meal. We have added fresh blueberries to these passover treats.

1 cup superfine sugar
1/2 cup vegetable oil
3 eggs
1/2 cup matzoh meal

2 tbsp. potato starch
1 tsp. cinnamon
1 3/4 cups blueberries

Preheat the oven to 350°F (175°C). Place 12 paper baking cups in a muffin pan.

In a medium bowl, beat the sugar, oil, and eggs with an electric mixer for 2 to 3 minutes. Set aside. In a small bowl, sift together the matzoh meal, potato starch, and cinnamon. Add the dry ingredients to the egg mixture. Stir in the blueberries. Spoon the mixture into the cups.

Bake for 20 minutes. Remove pan from the oven and cool for 5 minutes. Then remove the cupcakes and cool on a rack.

Store in an airtight container for up to 3 days, or freeze for up to 3 months.

Makes 1 dozen

irish barm brack cupcakes

see variations page 217

Traditionally, a quarter and a ring are hidden in barm brack cakes. The person who finds the ring will soon be married and the person who finds the quarter will soon be wealthy.

1/2 cup (3 1/2 oz.) raisins
1/2 cup (3 1/2 oz.) golden raisins
1/2 cup (3 1/2 oz.) currants
1 cup brewed black tea
4 cups all-purpose flour
1 tsp. allspice

1/3 cup packed brown sugar
1 tsp. baking powder
Pinch of salt
1 egg
1/2 cup (1 stick) sweet butter, melted

In a large bowl, soak the dried fruits in the tea. Leave overnight or for a minimum of 6 hours.

Preheat the oven to 400°F (200°C). Grease a 12-hole muffin pan with a little oil.

Mix the dry ingredients in a large bowl. In a separate large bowl, mix the egg and butter. Add the soaked and strained fruit, and stir well. Fold in the flour mixture.

Spoon the mixture into the prepared pan. (Optional: Place a ring in one of the cakes, and a quarter in another.) Bake until the cupcakes are a dark golden color. Remove pan from the oven and cool for 5 minutes. Then remove the cupcakes and cool on a rack. Serve with sweet butter. Store in an airtight container for up to 5 days, or freeze for up to 3 months.

Makes 1 dozen

king cupcakes

see variations page 218

Our version of the classic Mardi Gras "king cake." The colors traditionally used on the cake represent justice, faith, and power.

for the cupcakes
1 cup (2 sticks) sweet butter, softened
1 cup superfine sugar
2 cups self-rising flour
4 eggs
1 tsp. vanilla extract

for the frosting
2 1/2 cups confectioners' sugar
2 tbsp. lemon juice
2 tbsp. gold-colored sugar
2 tbsp. green-colored sugar
2 tbsp. purple-colored sugar

Preheat the oven to 350°F (175°C). Place 18 paper baking cups in muffin pans. Combine all the cupcake ingredients in a large bowl and beat with an electric mixer until smooth and pale, about 2 to 3 minutes.

Spoon the batter into the cups. Bake for 20 minutes. Remove pans from the oven and cool for 5 minutes. Then remove the cupcakes and cool on a rack.

To make the frosting, sift the confectioners' sugar in a medium bowl. Slowly add the lemon juice until the mixture becomes firm but spreadable. Spread onto the cupcakes, and sprinkle with the colored sugar.

Store unfrosted in an airtight container for up to 3 days, or freeze for up to 3 months.

Makes 1 1/2 dozen

mini christmas tree cupcakes

see variations page 219

These fun and festive little cakes will look superb on your Christmas dessert table.

for the cupcakes
1 cup (2 sticks) sweet butter, softened
1 cup superfine sugar
2 cups self-rising flour
4 eggs
1 tsp. vanilla extract

for the frosting
2 oz. ready-rolled white fondant frosting
2 oz. ready-rolled green fondant frosting
2 tbsp. raspberry jam
Colored candy balls

Preheat the oven to 350°F (175°C). Place 18 paper mini baking cups in muffin pans. Dust 2 cookie sheets with confectioners' sugar. Combine all the cupcake ingredients into a large bowl and beat with an electric mixer until smooth and pale, about 2 to 3 minutes. Spoon the batter into the cups. Bake for 20 minutes. Remove pans from the oven and cool for 5 minutes. Then remove the cupcakes and cool on a rack. To make the frosting, roll the white fondant frosting to 1/8 in. (3 mm) thick. Cut 18 circles using a 1 3/4-in. (4 1/2-cm) cookie cutter and set them on one of the cookie sheets. Roll the green fondant frosting to 1/8 in. (3 mm) thick. Using a small Christmas tree cookie cutter, cut shapes out of the frosting and place them on the other cookie sheet to firm a little. Brush each cupcake with a little raspberry jam, then place a white fondant disc on top. Top with a Christmas tree and decorate with the colored balls. Store unfrosted in an airtight container for up to 3 days, or freeze for up to 3 months.

Makes 1 1/2 dozen

christmas snowflake cupcakes

see variations page 220

These cupcakes are delightful for a Christmas gathering. You can serve them on Christmas Eve when Santa's sleigh has set off and the kids are tucked into bed.

for the cupcakes
1 cup (2 sticks) sweet butter, softened
1 cup superfine sugar
2 cups self-rising flour
4 eggs
1 tsp. vanilla extract

for the frosting
1/2 cup (1 stick) sweet butter, softened
2 cups confectioners' sugar, sifted
1 tsp. vanilla extract
2 tsp. pale dry sherry
4 tbsp. sweetened coconut

Preheat the oven to 350°F (175°C). Place 18 paper baking cups in muffin pans. Combine all the cupcake ingredients in a large bowl and beat with an electric mixer until smooth and pale, about 2 to 3 minutes.

Spoon the batter into the cups. Bake for 20 minutes. Remove pans from the oven and cool for 5 minutes. Then remove the cupcakes and cool on a rack.

For the frosting, beat the butter, confectioners' sugar, vanilla, and sherry in a medium bowl until smooth and creamy. Spread on top of the cupcakes. Sprinkle a little coconut on top to resemble snowflakes.

Store unfrosted in an airtight container for up to 3 days, or freeze for up to 3 months.

Makes 1 1/2 dozen

independence day cupcakes

see variations page 221

With their red, white, and blue frosting, these cupcakes make for a festive Fourth of July!

for the cupcakes
1 cup (2 sticks) sweet butter, softened
1 cup superfine sugar
2 cups self-rising flour
4 eggs
1 tsp. vanilla extract

for the frosting
1/2 cup (1 stick) sweet butter, softened
2 cups confectioners' sugar, sifted
1 tsp. vanilla extract
2 oz. ready-rolled white fondant frosting
2 oz. ready-rolled blue fondant frosting
2 oz. ready-rolled red fondant frosting

Preheat the oven to 350°F (175°C). Place 18 paper baking cups in muffin pans. Combine all the cupcake ingredients in a large bowl and beat with an electric mixer until smooth and pale, about 2 to 3 minutes. Spoon the batter into the cups. Bake for 20 minutes. Remove pans from the oven and cool for 5 minutes. Then remove the cupcakes and cool on a rack.

To make the frosting, beat the butter and confectioners' sugar until soft. Add the vanilla and beat again. Spread onto the cooled cupcakes. Roll the white fondant to 1/8 in. (3 mm) thick. Cut 18 circles using a 2 1/2-in. (6-cm) cookie cutter. Lay on top of the frosted cupcakes. Roll the red fondant to 1/8 in. (3 mm) thick. Cut small stars and lay on top of the white circles. Repeat for the blue fondant. Cut long 1/4-in. (6-mm) strips of both red and blue to make stripes. If strips are too short, join them by lightly pressing with a rolling pin. Add to the circles and stars. Store unfrosted in an airtight container for up to 3 days.

Makes 1 1/2 dozen

love-heart cupcakes

see variations page 222

These cupcakes make a delightful romantic gift for your true love on Valentine's Day — don't forget to attach a lover's message!

for the cupcakes
1 cup (2 sticks) sweet butter, softened
1 cup superfine sugar
2 cups self-rising flour
4 eggs
1 tsp. vanilla extract

for the frosting
2 oz. ready-rolled red fondant frosting
2 oz. ready-rolled white fondant frosting
3 tbsp. raspberry jam
Silver candy balls

Preheat the oven to 350°F (175°C). Dust two cookie sheets with confectioners' sugar and put aside. Place 18 paper baking cups in muffin pans. Combine all the cupcake ingredients in a large bowl and beat with an electric mixer until smooth and pale, about 2 to 3 minutes. Spoon the batter into the cups. Bake for 20 minutes. Remove pans from the oven and cool for 5 minutes. Then remove cupcakes and cool on a rack.

To make the frosting, roll the white fondant frosting to 1/8 in. (3 mm) thick. Cut 18 circles using a 2 1/2-in. (6-cm) cookie cutter, and set them on one of the cookie sheets. Roll the red fondant frosting to 1/8 in. (3 mm) thick. Using a heart-shaped cutter, cut out 18 small hearts and set them on the other cookie sheet. Brush each cupcake with a little jam and lay a white circle on top. Place a heart on top of the circle. Decorate with silver balls around the edge. Store unfrosted in an airtight container for up to 3 days, or freeze for up to 3 months.

Makes 1 1/2 dozen

birthday cupcakes

see variations page 223

This is an easy and fun way to personalize birthday cupcakes!

for the cupcakes
1 cup (2 sticks) sweet butter, softened
1 cup superfine sugar
2 cups self-rising flour
4 eggs
1 tsp. vanilla extract

for the frosting
1/2 cup (1 stick) sweet butter, softened
2 cups confectioners' sugar, sifted
1 tsp. vanilla extract
2 oz. ready-rolled white fondant frosting
2 oz. ready-rolled blue fondant frosting
2 oz. ready-rolled red fondant frosting
Silver candy balls

Preheat the oven to 350°F (175°C). Place 18 paper baking cups in muffin pans. Combine all the cupcake ingredients in a large bowl and beat with an electric mixer until smooth and pale, about 2 to 3 minutes. Spoon the batter into the cups. Bake for 20 minutes. Remove pans from the oven and cool for 5 minutes. Then remove the cupcakes and cool on a rack.

For the frosting, beat the butter and confectioners' sugar in a medium bowl until soft and creamy. Add the vanilla and beat again. Spread onto the cooled cupcakes. Roll the white fondant to 1/8 in. (3 mm) thick. Cut 18 circles using a 2 1/2-in. (6-cm) cookie cutter. Lay on top of the frosted cupcakes. Roll the red and blue fondant to 1/8 in. (3 mm) thick. Using mini alphabet cookie cutters, cut out initials and decorate the cupcakes. Garnish with silver balls. Store unfrosted in an airtight container for up to 3 days, or freeze for up to 3 months.

Makes 1 1/2 dozen

variations

st. patrick's day muffins

see base recipe page 193

scallion muffins
Prepare the basic muffin recipe, adding 3 tablespoons sliced scallions to the buttermilk mixture.

cabbage & caraway muffins
Prepare the basic muffin recipe, substituting 1/2 cup cooked cabbage and 1 teaspoon caraway seeds for the herbs.

bacon muffins
Prepare the basic muffin recipe, folding 3 tablespoons chopped, cooked bacon along with the potatoes.

variations

easter egg nests

see base recipe page 194

silver egg nests
Prepare the basic cupcake recipe, substituting 54 silver candy-coated almonds for the candy eggs.

orange-flavored egg nests
Prepare the basic cupcake recipe, adding 1 teaspoon orange extract to the chocolate frosting.

chocolate chip egg nests
Prepare the basic cupcake recipe, folding 1/2 cup (3 1/2 oz.) semisweet chocolate chips to the creamed batter.

variations

wedding cupcakes

see base recipe page 197

primrose wedding cupcakes
Prepare the basic cupcake recipe, substituting 18 frosted primroses
for the roses.

chocolate wedding cupcakes
Prepare the basic cupcake recipe, folding 1/2 cup (3 1/2 oz.) semisweet
chocolate chips into the creamed batter.

amaretto wedding cupcakes
Drizzle 3 tablespoons Amaretto over the cooled cupcakes before
frosting them.

halloween pumpkin muffins

see base recipe page 198

raisin & pumpkin muffins
Prepare the basic muffin recipe, adding 1/2 cup (3 1/2 oz.) raisins after folding the flour mixture into the pumpkin mixture.

ginger & pumpkin muffins
Prepare the basic muffin recipe, adding 1/2 cup (3 1/2 oz.) chopped candied ginger after folding the flour mixture into the pumpkin mixture.

pecan & pumpkin muffins
Prepare the basic muffin recipe, adding 1/2 cup (3 1/2 oz.) chopped pecans after folding the flour mixture into the pumpkin mixture.

variations

passover cupcakes

see base recipe page 200

cranberry passover cupcakes
Prepare the basic cupcake recipe, substituting 1 3/4 cups fresh cranberries for the blueberries.

orange & raisin passover cupcakes
Prepare the basic cupcake recipe, substituting 1/2 cup (3 1/2 oz.) raisins for the blueberries. Add 1 teaspoon orange extract to the egg mixture.

lemon & ginger passover cupcakes
Prepare the basic cupcake recipe, substituting 1 tablespoon lemon zest and 3 tablespoons chopped candied ginger for the blueberries.

irish barm brack cupcakes

see base recipe page 201

sugar-glazed barm brack cupcakes

Prepare the basic cupcake recipe. Prepare a glaze by mixing 2 tablespoons boiling water with 1 tablespoon superfine sugar. Brush the glaze on the cupcakes while they are still warm in the pan. Return the pan to the oven for a few minutes to allow the glaze to set and turn a shiny brown.

whiskey-glazed barm brack cupcakes

Prepare the basic cupcake recipe. Prepare a glaze by mixing 2 tablespoons warm Irish Whiskey with 1 tablespoon superfine sugar. Brush the glaze on the cupcakes while they are still warm in the pan. Return the pan to the oven for a few minutes to allow the glaze to set and turn a shiny brown.

apricot barm brack cupcakes

Prepare the basic cupcake recipe, adding 1/2 cup (3 1/2 oz.) chopped dried apricots to the dried fruit mixture. Increase quantity of black tea to 1 1/4 cups.

variations

king cupcakes

see base recipe page 203

raisin king cupcakes
Prepare the basic cupcake recipe, folding 1/2 cup (3 1/2 oz.) golden raisins into the creamed batter.

walnut king cupcakes
Prepare the basic cupcake recipe, folding 1/2 cup (3 1/2 oz.) chopped walnuts into the creamed batter.

white chocolate king cupcakes
Prepare the basic cupcake recipe, folding 1/2 cup (3 1/2 oz.) white chocolate chips into the creamed batter.

mini christmas tree cupcakes

see base recipe page 204

ginger & raisin christmas tree cupcakes
Prepare the basic cupcake recipe, adding 2 teaspoons ground ginger to the cupcake ingredients, and folding 1/2 cup (3 1/2 oz.) raisins into the creamed batter.

orange & lemon christmas tree cupcakes
Prepare the basic cupcake recipe, adding 1 tablespoon grated orange zest and 1 tablespoon grated lemon zest to the creamed batter.

white chocolate christmas tree cupcakes
Prepare the basic cupcake recipe, folding 1/2 cup (3 1/2 oz.) white chocolate chips into the creamed batter.

variations

christmas snowflake cupcakes

see base recipe page 206

poppy seed snowflake cupcakes
Prepare the basic cupcake recipe, adding 2 tablespoons poppy seeds to the creamed batter.

mixed berry snowflake cupcakes
Prepare the basic cupcake recipe, folding 4 tablespoons dried mixed cranberries, cherries, and blueberries into the creamed batter.

hazelnut snowflake cupcakes
Prepare the basic cupcake recipe, folding 3 tablespoons roasted chopped hazelnuts into the creamed batter.

independence day cupcakes

see base recipe page 207

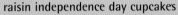

raisin independence day cupcakes

Prepare the basic cupcake recipe, folding 1/2 cup (3 1/2 oz.) raisins into the creamed batter.

white chocolate independence day cupcakes

Prepare the basic cupcake recipe, folding 1/2 cup (3 1/2 oz.) white chocolate chips into the creamed batter.

candied peel independence day cupcakes

Prepare the basic cupcake recipe, folding 2 tablespoons chopped candied peel into the creamed batter.

variations

love-heart cupcakes

see base recipe page 208

white chocolate heart cupcakes
Prepare the basic cupcake recipe, folding 1/2 cup (3 1/2 oz.) white chocolate chips into the creamed batter.

macadamia nut heart cupcakes
Prepare the basic cupcake recipe folding 1/2 cup (3 1/2 oz.) lightly toasted and chopped macadamia nuts into the creamed batter.

cherry heart cupcakes
Prepare the basic cupcake recipe folding 4 tablespoons chopped candied cherries into the creamed batter.

birthday cupcakes

see base recipe page 211

cherry & almond birthday cupcakes
Prepare the basic cupcake recipe, folding 2 tablespoons chopped
candied cherries and 2 tablespoons chopped blanched almonds into
the creamed batter.

orange birthday cupcakes
Prepare the basic cupcake recipe, adding 1 teaspoon orange extract to
the creamed batter.

candied fruit birthday cupcakes
Prepare the basic cupcake recipe, folding 3 tablespoons chopped candied
citrus fruits into the creamed batter.

cupcakes for kids

Crisp rice cupcakes and mini peanut butter cupcakes are a great

way to get kids involved in the kitchen. These cupcakes are so

much fun to decorate, it can be a party in itself!

s'more cupcakes

see variations page 247

Building s'more cupcakes is great fun for everyone. They require little fuss and effort, with a quick assembly and baking time.

24 graham crackers
1 cup (7 oz.) semisweet chocolate bars, broken
   into 12 squares

1/2 cup (3 1/2 oz.) chopped walnuts
3 tbsp. sweetened coconut
1 cup (2 oz.) mini marshmallows

Preheat the oven to 325°C (160°C). Place 12 paper baking cups in a muffin pan. Lay a cracker in the bottom of each cup. Add a piece of chocolate, followed by a sprinkle of walnuts and coconut. Lay another cracker on top.

Bake for 7 minutes, until the chocolate has melted. Remove pan from the oven. Push the cracker "lids" down so that they are secure.

Pop a couple of marshmallows on top of each cupcake. Return pan to the oven for 10 minutes, until the marshmallows melt and brown slightly.

Remove pan from the oven and cool for 5 minutes. Remove the cupcakes and cool on a rack.

Store in an airtight container for up to 24 hours.

Makes 1 dozen

toadstool cupcakes

see variations page 248

These funky toadstool cupcakes will brighten up any children's party.

for the cupcakes
1 cup (2 sticks) sweet butter, softened
1 cup superfine sugar
2 cups self-rising flour
1 tsp. baking powder
4 eggs
1 tsp. vanilla extract

for the frosting
3 cups confectioners' sugar, sifted
1 cup (2 sticks) sweet butter, softened
Pinch of salt
Red food coloring
2 oz. ready-rolled white fondant frosting

Preheat the oven to 350°F (175°C). Place 18 paper baking cups in muffin pans. Combine all the cupcake ingredients in a large bowl and beat with an electric mixer until smooth and pale, about 2 to 3 minutes. Spoon the batter into the cups. Bake for 20 minutes. Remove pans from the oven and cool for 5 minutes. Then remove the cupcakes and cool on a rack.

To make the frosting, cream the confectioners' sugar, butter, and salt in a medium bowl with an electric mixer until smooth. Add a few drops of the food coloring, and mix until the frosting is a uniform bright red. Cut small circles out of the fondant icing. Spoon the red frosting onto the cupcakes and place the white fondant circles on top.

Store unfrosted in an airtight container for up to 3 days, or freeze for up to 3 months.

Makes 1 1/2 dozen

ice cream cone cupcakes

see variations page 249

These cupcakes look like ice cream — but they won't melt!

for the cupcakes
1 cup (2 sticks) sweet butter, softened
1 cup superfine sugar
2 cups self-rising flour
1 tsp. baking powder
4 eggs
1 tsp. vanilla extract
24 mini flat-bottomed wafer cups

for the frosting
1 1/2 cups confectioners' sugar, sifted
1/4 cup (1/2 stick) sweet butter, softened
Pinch of salt
1/2 cup heavy cream
1 tsp. vanilla extract
2 tbsp. colored sprinkles

Preheat the oven to 350°F (175°C). Line a 24-cup mini muffin pan with paper baking cups. Combine all the cupcake ingredients in a large bowl and beat with an electric mixer until smooth and pale, about 2 to 3 minutes. Spoon the batter into the cups. Bake for 20 minutes. Remove pan from the oven and cool for 5 minutes. Then remove the cupcakes and cool on a rack. Peel off the paper baking cases, and place the cupcakes inside the ice cream cones.

To make the frosting, beat the confectioners' sugar, butter, and salt using an electric mixer. Add the cream and vanilla, and beat until smooth. Pipe the mixture in a swirl on top of the cupcake. Shake some sprinkles on top.

Store without frosting in an airtight container for up to 2 days.

Makes 2 dozen

think pink cupcakes

see variations page 250

Think pink while you're frosting and you will have a whole manner of colored cupcakes!

for the cupcakes
1 cup (2 sticks) sweet butter, softened
1 cup superfine sugar
2 cups self-rising flour
1 tsp. baking powder
4 eggs
1 tsp. vanilla extract

for the frosting
3 cups confectioners' sugar, sifted
1 cup (2 sticks) sweet butter, softened
Pinch of salt
Pink food coloring
Silver candy balls

Preheat the oven to 350°F (175°C). Place 18 paper baking cups in muffin pans. Combine all the cupcake ingredients in a large bowl and beat with an electric mixer until smooth and pale, about 2 to 3 minutes.

Spoon the batter into the cups. Bake for 20 minutes. Remove pans from the oven and cool for 5 minutes. Then remove the cupcakes and cool on a rack.

To make the frosting, cream the confectioners' sugar, butter, and salt with an electric mixer until smooth. Add a few drops of food coloring, and mix well. Spread the frosting liberally onto the cooled cupcakes and sprinkle with silver balls.

Store unfrosted in an airtight container for up to 3 days, or freeze for up to 3 months.

Makes 1 1/2 dozen

cookies & cream cupcakes

see variations page 251

Mix crushed cookies into the batter to give a crispy crunch to these cupcakes.

for the cupcakes
1 cup (2 sticks) sweet butter, softened
1 cup superfine sugar
2 cups self-rising flour
1 tsp. baking powder
4 eggs
1 tsp. vanilla extract
10 crushed cream-filled chocolate cookies

for the frosting
3 cups confectioners' sugar, sifted
1 cup (2 sticks) sweet butter, softened
Pinch of salt
10 chopped cream-filled chocolate cookies

Preheat the oven to 350°F (175°C). Place 18 foil or paper baking cups in muffin pans. Combine all the cupcake ingredients, except the cookies, in a large bowl and beat with an electric mixer until smooth and pale, about 2 to 3 minutes. Stir in the cookies.

Spoon the batter into the cups. Bake for 20 minutes. Remove pans from the oven and cool for 5 minutes. Then remove the cupcakes and cool on a wire rack.

To make the frosting, beat the confectioners' sugar, butter, and salt using an electric mixer. Spread the frosting onto the cooled cupcakes and sprinkle the chopped cookies on top.

Store unfrosted in an airtight container for up to 3 days, or freeze for up to 3 months.

Makes 1 1/2 dozen

alphabet cupcakes

see variations page 252

Line these up to spell somebody's name at a birthday party!

for the cupcakes
1 cup (2 sticks) sweet butter, softened
1 cup superfine sugar
2 cups self-rising flour
1 tsp. baking powder
4 eggs
1 tsp. vanilla extract

for the frosting
2 oz. ready-rolled white fondant frosting
3 tbsp. raspberry jam
2 oz. ready-rolled red, green, and black fondant
    frosting
Colored sprinkles

Preheat the oven to 350˚F (175˚C). Place 18 paper baking cups in muffin pans. Combine all the cupcake ingredients in a large bowl and beat with an electric mixer until smooth and pale, about 2 to 3 minutes. Spoon the batter into the cups. Bake for 20 minutes. Remove pans from the oven and cool for 5 minutes. Then remove the cupcakes and cool on a rack. For the frosting, roll out the white fondant and cut 18 circles using a 2-in. (5-cm) cookie cutter. Brush the cupcakes with a little of the jam. Press the circles onto the cupcakes. Using mini alphabet cutters, cut letter shapes from the colored fondant frosting and place them on top of the white circles. Sprinkle the edges with colored sprinkles.

Store unfrosted in an airtight container for up to 3 days, or freeze for up to 3 months.

Makes 1 1/2 dozen

pineapple cupcakes

see variations page 253

These cupcakes melt in the mouth and are the perfect teatime treat. Serve with a cup of Earl Grey tea.

for the cupcakes
1 cup (2 sticks) sweet butter, softened
1 cup superfine sugar
2 cups self-rising flour
1 tsp. baking powder
4 eggs
1 tsp. vanilla extract
1 cup drained crushed pineapple

for the frosting
1 cup cream cheese, softened
1 1/2 cups confectioners' sugar, sifted
1 tbsp. lemon juice
1 tsp. vanilla extract
1/2 cup (3 1/2 oz.) chopped walnuts

Preheat the oven to 350°F (175°C). Place 18 paper baking cups in muffin pans. Combine all the cupcake ingredients, except the pineapple, in a large bowl and beat with an electric mixer for about 2 to 3 minutes. Stir in the pineapple. Spoon the batter into the cups. Bake for 20 minutes. Remove pans from the oven and cool for 5 minutes. Then remove the cupcakes and cool on a rack. To make the frosting, slowly beat the cream cheese and confectioners' sugar in a large bowl with an electric mixer until creamy and soft. Add the lemon juice and vanilla, and beat briskly until well combined. Spread the frosting onto the cooled cupcakes and garnish with the chopped walnuts.

Store unfrosted in an airtight container for 2 to 3 days, or freeze for up to 3 months.

Makes 1 1/2 dozen

mini peanut butter cupcakes

see variations page 254

Simple and no fuss. You can make these cupcakes in large batches, which makes them ideal for kids' parties and picnics.

2 1/2 cups (2 oz.) milk chocolate
2 tbsp. sweet butter
3 tbsp. heavy cream
1 cup (6 oz.) smooth peanut butter

Place 12 mini foil baking cups in a muffin pan.

Place the chocolate, butter, and cream in a double boiler or in a medium bowl over a pan of simmering water, and stir until smooth. Remove from the heat and set aside.

With damp hands, shape the peanut butter into 12 small flat circles. Push the peanut butter into the bottom of the cups.

Pour the melted chocolate over the peanut butter, and refrigerate for at least 2 hours.

Store in an airtight container for up to 3 days.

Makes 1 dozen

crisp rice cupcakes

see variations page 255

I'm not too sure how many will reach the table, but these simple no-bake cupcakes are great
fun for the budding young chef to try.

1 cup (7 oz.) bittersweet chocolate
1/4 cup (1/2 stick) sweet butter, softened
5 tbsp. corn syrup
3 cups (3 1/2 oz.) crisp rice cereal

Place 12 foil or paper baking cups on a tray.

Place the chocolate and butter in a double boiler or in a medium bowl over a pan
of simmering water, and stir until melted.

Remove pan from the heat and stir in the cereal and corn syrup. Drop spoonfuls
of the mixture into the cups.

Refrigerate for 1 hour.

Store in an airtight container for up to 5 days.

Makes 1 dozen

eggy cupcakes

see variations page 256

Don't worry — you won't have to crack whole eggs to get this lovely sunny-side-up look.
Serve these cupcakes for breakfast with a glass of freshly squeezed juice.

for the cupcakes
1 cup (2 sticks) sweet butter, softened
1 cup superfine sugar
2 cups self-rising flour
1 tsp. baking powder
4 eggs
1 tsp. vanilla extract

for the frosting
3 cups confectioners' sugar, sifted
1 cup (2 sticks) sweet butter, softened
Pinch of salt
18 drained canned peach halves

Preheat the oven to 350°F (175°C). Place 18 paper baking cups in muffin pans. Combine all
the cupcake ingredients in a large bowl and beat with an electric mixer until smooth and
pale, about 2 to 3 minutes. Spoon the batter into the cups. Bake for 20 minutes. Remove
pans from the oven and cool for 5 minutes. Then remove the cupcakes and cool on a rack.

To make the frosting, put the confectioners' sugar, butter, and salt in a large bowl and beat
with an electric mixer until smooth. Liberally spread the frosting onto the cooled cupcakes
and garnish each cupcake with a peach half.

Store unfrosted in an airtight container for up to 3 days, or freeze for up to 3 months.

Makes 1 1/2 dozen

chocolate berry cupcakes

see variations page 257

My good friend Beverley Glock gave me this recipe. She runs a company called "Splat," which organizes children's parties where both children and adults can bake.

for the cupcakes
1/2 cup fresh or thawed frozen blackberries
3 tbsp. water
1 cup superfine sugar
1 cup self-rising flour
1 tsp. baking powder
1/2 cup soft margarine

2 eggs
1 tbsp. Dutch-process cocoa powder

for the ganache
3/4 cup (5 oz.) bittersweet chocolate, broken
3/4 cup heavy cream
12 blackberries

Preheat the oven to 350°F (175°C). Line a 12-cup mini muffin pan with paper baking cups. Combine the blackberries, water, and 1/2 cup sugar in a small saucepan over low heat. Simmer for about 5 minutes, until the fruit starts to release its juices. Set aside to cool. Combine the rest of the ingredients in a medium bowl and beat with an electric mixer until pale and creamy, about 2 to 3 minutes. Spoon the batter into the cups. Spoon a little of the fruit on top. Bake for 20 minutes. Remove the pan and cool for 5 minutes. Then remove the cupcakes and cool on a rack. To make the ganache, melt the chocolate and cream in a double boiler over low heat, until glossy and smooth. Dollop a spoonful of ganache onto each cooled cupcake and top with a blackberry. Refrigerate until set.

Store in an airtight container for up to 2 days, or freeze without ganache for up to 3 months.

Makes 1 dozen small cupcakes

pop rocks cupcakes

see variations page 258

Try these for a kid's party and watch their faces as the candy explodes in their mouths!

for the cupcakes
1 cup (2 sticks) sweet butter, softened
1 cup superfine sugar
2 cups self-rising flour
1 tsp. baking powder
4 eggs
1 tsp. vanilla extract

for the frosting
1/2 cup (1 stick) sweet butter, softened
2 cups confectioners' sugar, sifted
1 tsp. vanilla extract
2 sachets fruit-flavored Pop Rocks

Preheat the oven to 350°F (175°C). Place 18 paper baking cups in muffin pans.

Combine all cupcake ingredients in a large bowl and beat with an electric mixer until smooth and pale, about 2 to 3 minutes. Spoon the batter into the cups. Bake for 20 minutes.

Remove pans from the oven and cool for 5 minutes. Then remove the cupcakes and cool on a rack.

To make the frosting, cream the butter, confectioners' sugar, and vanilla in a medium bowl until smooth. Smear onto the cupcakes and sprinkle with Pop Rocks candy.

Store unfrosted in an airtight container for up to 2 days, or freeze for up to 3 months.

Makes 1 1/2 dozen

jelly donut cupcakes

see variations page 259

These cupcakes aren't donuts, but I'm sure you'll see the likeness when you bite into one.

for the cupcakes
1 cup (2 sticks) sweet butter, softened
1 cup superfine sugar
2 cups self-rising flour
1 tsp. baking powder
4 eggs
1 tsp. vanilla extract
1/2 cup raspberry jelly or jam

for the frosting
1 cup cream cheese, softened
1 1/2 cups confectioners' sugar, sifted
1 tbsp. lemon juice
1 tsp. of vanilla extract

Preheat the oven to 350°F (175°C). Place 18 paper baking cups in muffin pans. Combine all the cupcake ingredients, except the jelly, in a large bowl and beat with an electric mixer, about 2 to 3 minutes. Spoon the batter into the cups. Bake for 20 minutes. Remove pans from the oven and cool for 5 minutes. Then remove the cupcakes and cool on a rack.

Slice the top off each cupcake, hollow out a small hole with a teaspoon and fill with the jelly. Replace the top. To make the frosting, slowly beat the cream cheese and confectioners' sugar in a large bowl with an electric mixer until creamy and soft. Add the lemon juice and vanilla, and beat briskly until well combined. Spread the frosting onto the cupcakes.

Store unfrosted in an airtight container for up to 2 days, or freeze for up to 3 months.

Makes 1 1/2 dozen

variations

s'more cupcakes

see base recipe page 225

pecan s'more cupcakes
Prepare the basic cupcake recipe, substituting 1/2 cup (3 1/2 oz.) roughly chopped pecans for the walnuts.

white chocolate s'more cupcakes
Prepare the basic cupcake recipe, substituting 1/4 cup (2 oz.) white chocolate chips for half the semisweet chocolate.

chocolate & raspberry s'more cupcakes
Prepare the basic cupcake recipe. Add 1/2 cup lightly crushed raspberries along with the coconut and walnuts.

variations

toadstool cupcakes

see base recipe page 227

koala bear cupcakes
Prepare the basic cupcake recipe. Omit the rolled fondant. Color the frosting with brown food coloring instead of red. Make a koala face on each cupcake: A chocolate-covered brazil nut for the nose, 2 walnut halves for ears, and 2 candy eyes.

sneaky snake cupcakes
Prepare the basic cupcake recipe. For the frosting, substitute 2 oz. green ready-rolled fondant frosting for the white fondant. Brush each cupcake with a little fruit jelly. Roll the green fondant thinly and, using a cookie cutter, cut 18 circles 2-1/2 in. (6-cm) across and place one on each cupcake. For the trees, cut 6 chocolate sticks into 3 sections 2-in. (5-cm) in length, and stand upright on the fondant frosting. Roll 2 oz. red fondant frosting into 18 sausages 6-in. (15-cm) in length. Curl the fondant around the chocolate "trees" and decorate with candy-eyes.

bling bling cupcakes
Prepare the basic cupcake recipe. Omit the rolled fondant. Decorate the red frosting on the cupcakes with silver and gold candy balls.

ice cream cone cupcakes

see base recipe page 228

chocolate-frosted cone cupcakes
Prepare the basic cupcake recipe. To the frosting, add 1/2 cup (3 1/2 oz.) chocolate chips along with the cream and vanilla.

choc & mint-frosted cone cupcakes
Prepare the basic cupcake recipe. To the frosting, add 1/2 cup (3 1/2 oz.) mint chocolate chips along with the cream. Substitute 1 teaspoon mint extract for the vanilla.

honey & cream-frosted cone cupcakes
Prepare the basic cupcake recipe. To the frosting, add 1/3 cup honey after creaming the confectioners' sugar and butter.

variations

think pink cupcakes

see base recipe page 231

azure cupcakes
Prepare the basic cupcake recipe. For the frosting, substitute blue food coloring for pink, and top with blue azure sugar crystals.

lavender sugar cupcakes
Prepare the basic cupcake recipe. For the frosting, substitute blue food coloring for pink. Make lavender sugar by combining 3 tablespoons lavender flowers and 3/4 cup superfine sugar in a food processor for about 2 minutes. Put the sugar in a cool dry place, and let the flavors mingle for about 2 hours. Sprinkle on top of the frosting.

rose sugar cupcakes
Prepare the basic cupcake recipe. Make rose-petal sugar by combining 3 tablespoons red rose petals and 3/4 cup superfine sugar in a food processor for about 2 minutes. Put the sugar in a cool dry place, and let the flavors mingle for about 2 hours. Sprinkle on top of the frosting.

cookies & cream cupcakes

see base recipe page 232

minted cookies & cream cupcakes
Prepare the basic cupcake recipe, using cream-filled mint chocolate cookies in both the cupcakes and the frosting.

graham crackers & cream cupcakes
Prepare the basic cupcake recipe, substituting 1/2 cup (3 1/2 oz.) crushed graham crackers for 10 cookies in the cupcakes, and another 1/2 cup (3 1/2 oz.) crushed graham crackers for the cookies in the frosting.

chocolate, nougat, & cream cupcakes
Prepare the basic cupcake recipe, substituting 1/2 cup (3 1/2 oz.) chopped Baby Ruth bars for 10 cookies in the cupcakes, and another 1/2 cup (3 1/2 oz.) chopped Baby Ruth bars for the cookies in the frosting.

variations

alphabet cupcakes

see base recipe page 234

white chocolate alphabet cupcakes
Prepare the basic cupcake recipe, adding 1/2 cup (3 1/2 oz.) white chocolate chips to the creamed batter.

raisin alphabet cupcakes
Prepare the basic cupcake recipe, adding 1/2 cup (3 1/2 oz.) raisins to the creamed batter.

number cupcakes
Prepare the basic cupcake recipe. Use mini number cookie cutters instead of alphabet cutters.

pineapple cupcakes

see base recipe page 235

kicked-up chili pineapple cupcakes
Prepare the basic cupcake recipe. Add 1 teaspoon seeded and finely chopped chili pepper to the creamed batter.

orange & pineapple cupcakes
Prepare the basic cupcake recipe. Add 2 tablespoons orange zest to the creamed batter.

coconut & pineapple cupcakes
Prepare the basic cupcake recipe. Add 1/2 cup (2 1/2 oz.) sweetened shredded coconut to the mixture after it has been creamed.

variations

mini peanut butter cupcakes

see base recipe page 236

mini marshmallow & peanut butter cupcakes
Prepare the basic cupcake recipe. Add 1 cup chopped large marshmallows
to the melted chocolate mixture.

mini coconut & peanut butter cupcakes
Prepare the basic cupcake recipe. Add 3 tablespoons sweetened coconut
to the melted chocolate.

mini jam & peanut butter cupcakes
Prepare the basic cupcake recipe. Place a teaspoon of your favorite fruit
jam into the bottom of the baking cups and top with the peanut butter
and then the chocolate.

crisp rice cupcakes

see base recipe page 239

marshmallow & crisp rice cupcakes
Prepare the basic cupcake recipe. Stir in 1/2 cup mini marshmallows along with the cereal.

raisins & crisp rice cupcakes
Prepare the basic cupcake recipe. Stir in 1/2 cup (3 1/2 oz.) raisins along with the cereal.

cherry & crisp rice cupcakes
Prepare the basic cupcake recipe. Stir in 1/2 cup (3 1/2 oz.) chopped red candied cherries along with the cereal.

variations

eggy cupcakes

see base recipe page 240

kiwi cupcakes
Prepare the basic cupcake recipe, substituting 18 thin slices kiwi fruit for the peach halves.

nectarine cupcakes
Prepare the basic cupcake recipe, substituting 18 nectarine halves for the peach halves.

custard (runny egg) cupcakes
Prepare the basic cupcake recipe. Slice a thin circle off the top of each cooled cupcake. Using a teaspoon, make a small hole about 1 in. (2 1/2 cm) deep. Pipe 1 teaspoon prepared custard into the hole. Replace the "lid," frost and add the peach half.

variations

chocolate berry cupcakes

see base recipe page 243

chocolate raspberry cupcakes
Prepare the basic cupcake recipe, substituting 1/2 cup fresh raspberries for
the blackberries.

chocolate blueberry cupcakes
Prepare the basic cupcake recipe, substituting 1/2 cup fresh blueberries for
the blackberries.

chocolate cherry cupcakes
Prepare the basic cupcake recipe, substituting 1/2 cup fresh cherries for
the blackberries.

variations

pop rocks cupcakes

see base recipe page 244

ginger pop rocks cupcakes
Prepare the basic cupcake recipe, adding 1 teaspoon ground ginger
and 3 tablespoons candied ginger to the creamed cupcake batter.

cherry pop rocks cupcakes
Prepare the basic cupcake recipe, adding 1/2 cup (3 1/2 oz.) chopped candied
cherries to the creamed cupcake batter.

pineapple pop rocks cupcakes
Prepare the basic cupcake recipe, adding 1/2 cup (3 1/2 oz.) chopped dried
pineapple to the creamed cupcake batter.

jelly donut cupcakes

see base recipe page 246

boston cream donut cupcakes
Prepare the basic cupcake recipe. Substitute 1/2 cup vanilla custard or pie filling for the raspberry jelly.

chocolate custard donut cupcakes
Prepare the basic cupcake recipe. Substitute 1/2 cup chocolate custard or pie filling for the raspberry jelly.

marmalade donut cupcakes
Prepare the basic cupcake recipe. Substitute 1/2 cup orange marmalade for the raspberry jelly.

wholesome muffins

This chapter is packed full of recipes filled with healthy,

good-for-you ingredients. From whole wheat peach muffins

to mini couscous cakes, being healthy never tasted so good!

spinach & pine nut muffins

see variations page 280

This is a wonderful Mediterranean combination and an ideal lunchtime treat.

2 1/3 cups all-purpose flour
Pinch of salt
1 tbsp. baking powder
2 tbsp. superfine sugar
1/4 tsp. nutmeg

1 1/4 cups milk
3 tbsp. olive oil
1 lightly beaten egg
1 cup chopped cooked spinach
1/2 cup (3 1/2 oz.) pine nuts

Preheat the oven to 350˚F (175˚C). Grease a large 6-cup muffin pan. Mix the dry ingredients in a medium bowl.

In a large bowl, combine the milk, oil, and egg with an electric mixer until well combined. Fold the flour mixture into the milk mixture and stir until nearly combined. Stir in the spinach and pine nuts.

Spoon the batter into the prepared pan. Bake for 20 minutes. Remove pan from the oven and cool for 5 minutes. Remove the muffins and cool on a rack.

Store in an airtight container for up to 3 days, or freeze for up to 3 months.

Makes 1/2 dozen muffins

wild rice muffins

see variations page 281

Wild rice is technically a marsh grass, with a fantastic nutty texture.

1/3 cup wild rice, soaked in cold water for
    about 2 hours
2 eggs
1 1/4 cups milk
1/2 cup (1 stick) sweet butter, melted
1 1/2 cups all-purpose flour
1/2 cup wheat bran

1/3 cup packed brown sugar
1 tbsp. baking powder
1/2 tsp. allspice
3 tbsp. chopped dried prunes
3 tbsp. chopped hazelnuts
4 tbsp. chopped dried peaches

Drain the wild rice. Place it in a medium saucepan, cover with 2 cups cold water, and bring to a boil. Simmer for 50 minutes, until the rice is tender. Drain and rinse under cold water. Set aside to cool.

Preheat the oven to 375°F (190°C). Grease a 12-cup muffin pan. In a medium bowl, beat the rice, eggs, milk, and butter with an electric mixer until combined. In a large bowl, combine the flour, bran, sugar, baking powder, and allspice. Add the cooled rice mixture and stir until just combined. Fold in the prunes, hazelnuts, and peaches. Spoon the mixture into the prepared pan. Bake for 20 minutes. Remove pan from the oven and cool for 5 minutes. Then remove muffins and cool on a rack.

Store in an airtight container for up to 3 days, or freeze for up to 3 months.

Makes 1 dozen

mini couscous cakes

see variations page 282

Couscous, the world's smallest pasta, is a staple throughout northern Africa. It gives these cakes a light and elegant texture.

1/2 cup couscous
1/2 cup boiling water
2 cups all-purpose flour
2 tbsp. superfine sugar
1 tbsp. baking powder
Pinch of salt

1 tsp. toasted cumin seeds
1 tsp. ground coriander
1 egg
4 tbsp. olive oil
1 tbsp. lemon zest
2 tbsp. chopped flat-leaf parsley

Preheat the oven to 350°F (175°C). Place 24 mini paper cups in a muffin pan. Put the couscous in a medium bowl and pour the boiling water over it. Cover and leave for 5 minutes, so the grains absorb the liquid. Fluff the grains apart with a fork.

Mix the dry ingredients in a bowl with a spoon. Beat the egg and oil in a large bowl with a an electric mixer until combined. Add the couscous and the dry ingredients and mix until nearly combined. Fold in the lemon zest and parsley. Spoon the mixture into the cups. Bake for 20 minutes. Remove pan from the oven and cool for 5 minutes. Then remove the mini cakes and cool on a rack.

Store in an airtight container for up to 3 days, or freeze for up to 3 months.

Makes 2 dozen mini cakes

basil pesto cupcakes

see variations page 283

These unusually savory cupcakes make an ideal wholesome treat.

for the cupcakes
3/4 cup yellow cornmeal
1 cup all-purpose flour
2 tsp. baking powder
3 tbsp. sugar
Pinch of salt
2 eggs
1 cup whole milk
4 tbsp. (1/2 stick) sweet butter, melted

for the frosting
1/2 cup basil pesto
1 1/2 cups cream cheese, softened
12 cherry tomatoes

Preheat the oven to 350°F (175°C). Place 12 paper baking cups into a muffin pan. In a medium bowl, stir the dry ingredients. Beat the eggs, milk, and butter in a large bowl with an electric mixer until combined. Add the flour mixture to the egg mixture, and stir until just combined. Spoon the batter into the cups. Bake for 20 minutes. Remove pan and cool for 5 minutes. Then remove the cupcakes and cool on a rack.

For the frosting, beat the pesto and cream cheese with an electric mixer until smooth and creamy. Smear the frosting onto the cooled cupcakes and top with the cherry tomatoes.

Store unfrosted in an airtight container for up to 3 days, or freeze for up to 3 months.

Makes 1 dozen

vegetable bran muffins

see variations page 284

These muffins are great for children because they contain a host of essential nutrients
and vitamins — and yet they taste delicious.

4 cups oat bran
1 cup self-rising flour
1 tsp. baking powder
1/2 cup packed brown sugar
Pinch of salt
2 tsp. cinnamon

2 cups milk
4 tbsp. vegetable oil
2 lightly beaten eggs
2 tbsp. honey
2 cups shredded zucchini & carrots
1 1/2 cups (9 oz.) raisins

Preheat the oven to 350°F (175°C). Grease a 12-cup muffin pan.

In a large bowl, combine the dry ingredients with a spoon. In a separate bowl, beat the milk,
oil, eggs, and honey with an electric mixer until combined. Stir in the shredded vegetables
and raisins. Add the dry ingredients and stir until just combined. Spoon the mixture into
the prepared pan.

Bake in the oven for 20 minutes. Remove pan from the oven and cool for 5 minutes. Then
remove the muffins and cool on a rack.

Store in an airtight container for up to 3 days, or freeze for up to 3 months.

Makes 1 dozen

whole wheat peach muffins

see variations page 285

Peaches are packed full of vitamins. They have high levels of vitamin A and beta carotene which help keep the immune system strong and combat the signs of aging.

2 cups drained stewed or canned peaches
1 1/2 cups all-purpose flour
3/4 cup whole wheat flour
2 tsp. baking powder
Pinch of salt

1/3 cup packed brown sugar
1 lightly beaten egg
4 tbsp. vegetable oil
1/2 cup whole milk

Preheat the oven to 350°F (175°C). Grease a large 6-cup muffin pan.

Purée the peaches in a food processor. In a medium bowl, combine the flours, baking powder, salt, and sugar with a spoon.

In a large bowl, beat the egg, oil, and milk with an electric mixer until combined. Stir in the peach purée, then add the flour mixture and mix until just combined. Spoon the mixture into the prepared pan. Bake for 20 minutes. Remove pan from the oven and cool for 5 minutes. Then remove the muffins and cool on a rack.

Store in an airtight container for up to 3 days, or freeze for up to 3 months.

Makes 1/2 dozen

oatmeal muffins

see variations page 286

These hearty muffins make a great start to the day. You won't feel hungry until lunchtime!

2 cups all-purpose flour
1 cup packed brown sugar
1 tbsp. baking powder
1 tsp. cinnamon
1/3 cup wheat bran
1/3 cup rolled oats

Pinch of salt
2 cups buttermilk
2 lightly beaten eggs
3/4 cup vegetable oil
1 cup (6 oz.) raisins

Preheat the oven to 350°F (175°C). Grease a 12-cup muffin pan.

In a medium bowl, combine the dry ingredients with a spoon. In a large bowl, beat the buttermilk, eggs, and oil with an electric mixer until combined.

Add the dry ingredients and stir until almost blended. Fold in the raisins.

Spoon the mixture into the prepared pan. Bake for 20 minutes. Remove pan from the oven and cool for 5 minutes. Then remove the muffins and cool on a rack.

Store in an airtight container for up to 2 days, or freeze for up to 3 months.

Makes 1 dozen

eggplant caviar muffins

see variations page 287

The caviar in the title actually refers to the eggplant seeds, or "eggs."

for the cupcakes
2 small eggplants
6 tbsp. extra virgin olive oil
2 1/2 cups all-purpose flour
4 tsp. baking powder
Pinch of salt
1 lightly beaten egg
1 1/4 cups milk

for the butter
1/2 cup (1 stick) sweet butter, softened
2 cloves finely minced garlic
2 tsp. sherry vinegar
Pinch of salt and pepper
1 tbsp. chopped parsley

Preheat the oven to 400°F (200°C). Rub the eggplants with 2 tablespoons olive oil. Bake on a cookie sheet for 30 minutes, until the eggplant softens and turns dark brown. When cool enough to handle, remove the tops and slice lengthwise. Using a spoon, scrape the flesh away from the skin. Discard the skin and roughly chop the eggplant flesh. Set aside.

Grease a 12-cup muffin pan. In a medium bowl, combine the dry ingredients. In a large bowl, beat the egg, milk, and remaining olive oil. Mix in the flour until nearly combined. Fold in the chopped eggplant. Spoon the mixture into the prepared pan. Bake for 25 minutes. Remove pan from the oven and cool for 5 minutes. Then remove the muffins and cool on a rack. To make the butter, combine the butter, garlic, vinegar, and parsley in a bowl. Beat until well combined, then season with salt and pepper. Serve as an accompaniment to the muffins. Store in an airtight container for up to 2 days, or freeze for up to 3 months.

Makes 1 dozen

pistachio & apricot muffins

see variations page 288

The pistachio is a highly prized nut used throughout the Mediterranean to flavor everything from patés to ice creams.

1 1/3 cups (8 oz.) roughly chopped dried
    apricots
4 tbsp. brandy
4 cups self-rising flour
1/2 cup (1 stick) sweet butter, cubed

3/4 cup superfine sugar
2 lightly beaten eggs
3/4 cup buttermilk
1/2 cup (3 1/2 oz.) chopped pistachios

Soak the chopped apricots in the brandy and let stand for 1 hour.

Preheat the oven to 350°F (175°C). Grease a 12-cup muffin pan. Drain the apricots and then purée in a food processor until smooth. Put the flour and butter in a medium bowl. Using your fingertips, cut in the butter with the flour until it resembles fine breadcrumbs. Stir in the sugar, eggs, buttermilk, and pistachios until just combined.

Spoon the mixture into the prepared pan. Bake for 20 minutes. Remove pan from the oven and cool for 5 minutes. Then remove the muffins and cool on a rack.

Store in an airtight container for up to 3 days, or freeze for up to 3 months.

Makes 1 dozen

pb & banana cupcakes

see variations page 289

This familiar combination makes a truly delicious cupcake.

1 cup (2 sticks) sweet butter, softened
1 cup superfine sugar
1 cup self-rising flour
1 cup self-rising whole wheat flour
1 tsp. baking powder
4 eggs
3 tbsp. ground almonds
1 tsp. vanilla extract
2 tsp. cinnamon

4 tbsp. peanut butter chips
1 cup (about 2) mashed bananas

for the frosting
1 cup cream cheese, softened
1 1/2 cups confectioners' sugar, sifted
1 tbsp. lemon juice
1 tsp. of vanilla extract
1/2 cup mashed banana

Preheat the oven to 350°F (175°C). Place 24 paper baking cups in muffin pans. Combine the butter, sugar, flours, baking powder, eggs, almonds, vanilla, and cinnamon in a large bowl and beat with an electric mixer until smooth and pale, about 2 to 3 minutes. Stir in the peanut butter chips and mashed bananas. Spoon the batter into the paper cups. Bake for 20 minutes. Remove pan and cool for 5 minutes. Then remove the cupcakes and cool on a rack.

To make the frosting, beat the cream cheese and confectioners' sugar in a medium bowl with an electric mixer until soft and light. Add the lemon juice, vanilla, and mashed bananas. Beat until well combined. Spoon the frosting over the cupcakes. Store in an airtight container for up to 2 days or freeze for up to 3 months.

Makes 2 dozen

chickpea muffins

see variations page 290

Chickpeas, or garbanzo beans, are full of fiber and make these muffins a great lunchtime treat.

3 tbsp. plus 1 1/4 cups cornmeal
2 1/3 cups self-rising flour
2 tbsp. chopped fresh basil
1 tsp. baking powder
Pinch of salt

1 1/3 cups milk
1 lightly beaten egg
1/3 cup sweet butter, melted
1 3/4 cups drained canned or cooked chickpeas
2 tbsp. shredded Parmesan cheese

Preheat the oven to 350°F (175°C). Grease a 6-cup muffin pan and dust with 3 tablespoons cornmeal. In a medium bowl, combine the flour, remaining cornmeal, basil, baking powder, and salt with a spoon. In a large bowl, beat the milk, egg, and butter with an electric mixer until combined. Add the chickpeas and Parmesan cheese. Add the flour mixture and stir until just combined. Spoon the mixture into the prepared pan. Bake for 25 minutes.

Remove pan and cool for 5 minutes. Then remove the muffins and cool on a rack.

Store in an airtight container for up to 3 days, or freeze for up to 3 months.

Makes 1/2 dozen

date & pecan muffins

see variations page 291

With over 40 different named varieties, the date fruit of the palm tree comes in many different textures and flavors. For this muffin try using Medjool dates, which have a thick flesh and a dark, rich flavor.

2 1/2 cups all-purpose flour
3/4 cup superfine sugar
1 tbsp. baking powder
2 eggs
4 tbsp. butter, melted

1/4 cup sour cream
2 tbsp. milk
1 large mashed banana
1 cup (6 oz.) chopped dates
4 tbsp. chopped pecans

Preheat the oven to 350°F (175°C). Grease a 12-cup muffin pan. In a medium bowl, combine the flour, sugar, and baking powder with a spoon.

In a large bowl, beat the eggs, butter, sour cream, milk, and banana with an electric mixer until combined. Fold in the flour mixture until just combined. Stir in the dates and pecan nuts.

Spoon the mixture into the prepared pan. Bake for 20 minutes. Remove pan from the oven and cool for 5 minutes. Then remove the muffins and cool on a rack.

Store in an airtight container for up to 3 days, or freeze for up to 3 months.

Makes 1 dozen

variations

spinach & pine nut muffins

see base recipe page 261

pesto & pine nut muffins

Prepare the basic muffin recipe, substituting 1/4 cup fresh basil pesto for the spinach.

spinach, pine nut, & black olive muffins

Prepare the basic muffin recipe, adding 1/4 cup finely chopped black olives along with the spinach and pine nuts.

spinach & parmesan muffins

Prepare the basic muffin recipe, mixing 4 tablespoons freshly shredded Parmesan cheese in with the spinach and pine nuts. Sprinkle 1/2 teaspoon Parmesan on top of each muffin before baking.

wild rice muffins

see base recipe page 262

wild rice & date muffins
Prepare the basic muffin recipe, substituting 3 tablespoons chopped dates for the chopped prunes.

wild rice & apricot muffins
Prepare the basic muffin recipe, substituting 4 tablespoons chopped dried apricots for the chopped peaches.

wild rice & berry muffins
Prepare the basic muffin recipe, substituting 1 1/2 tablespoons dried blueberries, 1 1/2 tablespoons dried cranberries, and 1 1/2 tablespoons dried cherries for the chopped peaches.

mini couscous cakes

see base recipe page 265

mini couscous & cilantro cakes
Prepare the basic cupcake recipe, adding 2 tablespoons freshly chopped cilantro along with the lemon zest and parsley.

mini couscous cakes with preserved lemon & thyme
Prepare the basic cupcake recipe, adding 1 teaspoon chopped preserved lemon and 1 tablespoon chopped thyme leaves along with the lemon zest and parsley.

mini couscous cakes with olive & chili
Prepare the basic cupcake recipe, adding 3 tablespoons tapenade or olive paste and 1 teaspoon chopped chili pepper along with the lemon zest and parsley.

basil pesto cupcakes

see base recipe page 266

basil pesto & cilantro cupcakes
Prepare the basic cupcake recipe, adding 3 tablespoons finely chopped cilantro to the frosting.

red pepper pesto cupcakes
Prepare the basic cupcake recipe, substituting 1/2 cup red pepper pesto for the basil pesto.

basil pesto & chili cupcakes
Prepare the basic cupcake recipe, adding 1 teaspoon chili flakes to the batter before it has been mixed together.

variations

vegetable bran muffins

see base recipe page 268

feta & vegetable bran muffins
Prepare the basic muffin recipe, folding in 1/4 cup crumbled feta cheese after adding the vegetables and raisins.

apple bran muffins
Prepare the basic muffin recipe, substituting 1 cup shredded apple for the shredded zucchini.

thyme bran muffins
Prepare the basic muffin recipe, adding 1 tablespoon fresh thyme along with the vegetables and raisins.

variations

whole wheat peach muffins

see base recipe page 269

whole wheat apricot muffins
Prepare the basic muffin recipe, substituting 2 cups fresh or canned apricot for the peaches.

whole wheat pear muffins
Prepare the basic muffin recipe, substituting 2 cups fresh or canned pears for the peaches.

whole wheat nectarine muffins
Prepare the basic muffin recipe, substituting 2 cups fresh or canned nectarines for the peaches.

variations

oatmeal muffins

see base recipe page 270

raspberry oatmeal muffins
Prepare the basic muffin recipe, substituting 1 cup (7 oz.) dried raspberries for the raisins.

blueberry oatmeal muffins
Prepare the basic muffin recipe, substituting 1 cup (7 oz.) dried blueberries for the raisins.

cranberry oatmeal muffins
Prepare the basic muffin recipe, substituting 1 cup (7 oz.) dried cranberries for the raisins.

eggplant caviar muffins

see base recipe page 273

red pepper & eggplant muffins
Prepare the basic muffin recipe, adding 3 tablespoons minced red pepper along with adding the eggplant.

raisin & cinnamon eggplant muffins
Prepare the basic muffin recipe, adding 1/2 cup (3 1/2 oz.) raisins and 2 teaspoons cinnamon along with the eggplant.

sesame seed & eggplant muffins
Prepare the basic muffin recipe, adding 3 tablespoons tahini paste before folding in the eggplant.

variations

pistachio & apricot muffins

see base recipe page 274

pecan & apricot muffins
Prepare the basic muffin recipe, substituting 3 tablespoons chopped pecans for the pistachios.

pistachio & peach muffins
Prepare the basic muffin recipe, substituting 1 1/3 cups (8 oz.) dried peaches for the apricots.

walnut & apricot muffins
Prepare the basic muffin recipe, substituting 3 tablespoons chopped walnuts for the pistachios.

variations

pb & banana cupcakes

see base recipe page 276

banana & pecan cupcakes
Prepare the basic cupcake recipe, substituting 4 tablespoons of chopped pecans for the peanut butter chips.

pb & banana cupcakes with maple syrup & ginger frosting
Prepare the basic cupcake recipe. In the frosting, substitute 4 tablespoons maple syrup for the confectioners' sugar. Stir in 3 tablespoons chopped candied ginger along with the peanut butter chips and mashed banana.

banana, peanut butter, & chocolate chip cupcakes
Prepare the basic cupcake recipe, adding 4 tablespoons of semisweet chocolate chips after creaming the batter.

variations

chickpea muffins

see base recipe page 277

mixed herb muffins
Prepare the basic muffin recipe, adding 1 tablespoon each chopped fresh
flat leaf parsley, fresh chives, and fresh thyme to the dry ingredients.

chili muffins
Prepare the basic muffin recipe, adding 1 teaspoon fresh chili flakes to
the dry ingredients.

roasted garlic butter muffins
Prepare the basic muffin recipe. Serve with roasted garlic butter. Mix
2 tablespoons minced roasted garlic with 1/2 cup (1 stick) sweet butter,
1 tablespoon chopped parsley, and 1 teaspoon lemon zest.

variations

date & pecan muffins

see base recipe page 278

date & pecan muffins with maple syrup butter
Prepare the basic muffin recipe and serve with orange and maple syrup butter. Mix 1 teaspoon orange extract with 2 tablespoons maple syrup. Combine with 1/2 cup (1 stick) softened, sweet butter.

date & pistachio muffins
Prepare the basic muffin recipe, substituting 4 tablespoons chopped pistachios for the pecans.

date & macadamia nut muffins
Prepare the basic muffin recipe, substituting 4 tablespoons chopped macadamia nuts for the pecans.

low-fat cupcakes

Moist and sweet banana and honey cupcakes, spicy and earthy

pumpkin and ginger muffins — you'll never know these flavorful

cupcakes are low in fat!

ricotta cheesecake cupcakes

see variations page 314

Ricotta cheese is lower in fat than cream cheese and it has a great texture.

1 cup graham cracker crumbs
3 tbsp. margarine, melted
2 tbsp. honey
4 cups part-skim ricotta cheese

4 eggs
1 1/2 cups confectioners' sugar, sifted
1 tsp. orange extract
1/2 cup (3 1/2 oz.) walnut halves

Preheat the oven to 325°F (160°C). Place 12 baking cups in a muffin pan.

In a food processor, combine the cracker crumbs, margarine, and honey. Spoon 1 tablespoon of the mixture into each cup, pressing firmly into the bottom. Chill until set.

In a large bowl, beat the ricotta with an electric mixer until soft. Then beat in the eggs, confectioners' sugar, and orange extract. Fold in the walnuts. Spoon the mixture into the cups.

Bake for 25 minutes. Remove pan from the oven and cool for 5 minutes. Then remove the cupcakes and cool on a rack. Chill until ready to serve.

Store covered in the refrigerator for up to 2 days.

Makes 1 dozen

raspberry & cottage cheese muffins

see variations page 315

These muffins make a delicious treat whether you are counting fat grams or not!

2 1/3 cups all-purpose flour
3/4 cup superfine sugar
1 tbsp. baking powder
Pinch of salt
2 lightly beaten eggs

4 tbsp. sunflower oil
1 1/4 cups low-fat milk
1/2 cup low-fat cottage cheese
2 cups fresh raspberries

Preheat the oven to 350°F (175°C). Grease a 12-cup muffin pan.

In a medium bowl, mix the flour, sugar, baking powder, and salt with a spoon.

In a large bowl, beat the eggs, oil, milk, and cottage cheese with an electric mixer until smooth. Add the flour mixure and stir until nearly combined. Fold in the raspberries, but do not overmix. Spoon the mixture into prepared pan. Bake in the oven for 20 minutes.

Remove pan from the oven and cool for 5 minutes. Then remove the muffins and cool on a rack. Store in an airtight container for up to 2 days, or freeze for up to 3 months.

Makes 1 dozen

low-fat chocolate chip muffins

see variations page 316

These low-fat chocolate treats won't tip the balance on the scales.

for the muffins
2 2/3 cups all-purpose flour
1 cup superfine sugar
1 tbsp. baking powder
2 tbsp. Dutch-process cocoa powder
2 lightly beaten eggs
1/2 cup sunflower oil
3/4 cup fat-free milk
1 tsp. vanilla extract

for the frosting
2 tbsp. margarine, softened
1 1/2 cups confectioners' sugar, sifted
1/3 cup Dutch-process cocoa powder
1/2 tsp. orange extract
1/2 tsp. vanilla extract
4 tbsp. fat-free milk

Preheat the oven to 350°F (175°C). Grease a 12-cup muffin pan. In a medium bowl, mix the flour, sugar, baking powder, and cocoa with a spoon. In a large bowl, combine the eggs, oil, milk, and vanilla with an electric mixer and beat until combined. Add the flour mixture and stir until just combined. Do not overmix. Spoon the batter into the prepared pan. Bake for 20 minutes. Remove pan from the oven and cool for 5 minutes. Then remove the muffins and cool on a rack. For the frosting, combine all the ingredients except the milk. Add the milk slowly, beating with an electric mixer to make a firm but spreadable mixture. Spoon the frosting onto the cooled muffins.

Store unfrosted in an airtight container for up to 3 days, or freeze for up to 3 months.

Makes 1 dozen

low-fat vanilla cupcakes

see variations page 317

After you have used the seeds from the vanilla bean, put the pod into an airtight jar and pour superfine sugar on top. In a few weeks you will have vanilla sugar!

for the cupcakes
3 egg yolks
1 cup superfine sugar
1 vanilla bean, pod removed
1/4 cup cold water
1 cup cake flour
1 tsp. baking powder
Pinch of salt

5 egg whites
1/8 tsp. cream of tartar

for the glaze
1 1/2 cups confectioners' sugar
1 tsp. vanilla extract
2 tbsp. lemon juice
1 tbsp. poppy seeds

Preheat the oven to 350°F (175°C). Place 12 paper baking cups in a muffin pan. In a large bowl, beat the egg yolks and half the sugar until pale and creamy. Then add the vanilla seeds. Add the water, flour, baking powder and salt to the egg mixture and beat with an electric mixer until just combined. In a medium bowl, combine the egg whites and cream of tartar. Beat with an electric mixer until soft peaks form. Add the remaining sugar, one-third at a time, beating well after each addition. Using a metal spoon, gently fold the egg whites into the batter. Spoon the mixture into the cups. Bake for 20 minutes. To make the glaze, sift the confectioners' sugar in a bowl. Add the vanilla extract, lemon juice, and poppy seeds and beat until creamy and slightly runny. Drizzle the glaze over the cupcakes. Store in an airtight container for up to 2 days, or freeze for up to 3 months.

Makes 1 dozen

flour-lite chocolate cupcakes

see variations page 318

This recipe has only a small amount of flour to give the cupcakes a light, fluffy texture.

1/2 cup Dutch-process cocoa powder
3/4 cup packed light brown sugar
3 tbsp. all-purpose flour
Pinch of salt
1 tsp. vanilla extract
1 tsp. orange extract
3/4 cup fat-free milk

1 cup chopped bittersweet chocolate
1 lightly beaten egg
3 egg whites
1/4 tsp. cream of tartar
1/3 cup superfine sugar
Cocoa powder, for dusting
Confectioners' sugar, for dusting

In a heavy saucepan, combine the cocoa, sugar, flour, salt, vanilla, orange extract, and milk over a gentle heat. Stir until the sugar dissolves, being careful not to burn the mixture. Remove from the heat, and gradually stir in the chocolate until it melts. Whisk in the egg. Transfer to a large bowl to cool, and set aside. Preheat the oven to 350°F (175°C). Place 12 paper baking cups in a muffin pan. In a medium bowl, combine the egg whites and cream of tartar. Beat with an electric mixer until soft peaks form. Gradually add the sugar, one-third at a time, beating for 1 minute after each addition. Using a metal spoon, fold the egg whites into the chocolate, making sure not to overmix. Spoon the mixture into the cups. Bake for 20 minutes. Remove the pan from the oven and cool for 5 minutes. Then remove the cupcakes, dust with cocoa powder and confectioners' sugar, and serve immediately.

Store in an airtight container for up to 2 days, or freeze for up to 3 months.

Makes 1 dozen

quick applesauce cupcakes

see variations page 319

Simple to make and low in fat, this recipe is based on the classic streusel cake.

for the cupcakes
1/2 cup (1 stick) margarine, softened
3/4 cup packed light brown sugar
1 lightly beaten egg
3/4 cup unsweetened applesauce
2 cups self-rising flour
1 tsp. baking powder
1 tsp. ground ginger
1/4 tsp. ground cloves

for the topping
2 tbsp. margarine, softened
1/4 cup confectioners' sugar, sifted
3 tbsp. chopped walnuts
2 tbsp. rolled oats
2 tbsp. all-purpose flour
1/2 tsp. cinnamon

Preheat the oven to 350°F (175°C). Place 12 paper baking cups in a muffin pan. In a medium bowl, beat the margarine and sugar with an electric mixer until pale and creamy. Slowly add the egg and then the applesauce, beating well after each addition. Add the flour, baking powder, and spices, mixing until just combined. To make the topping, combine all the ingredients in a small bowl. Mix with a fork until the topping resembles coarse breadcrumbs. Set aside. Spoon the batter into the cups. Sprinkle some topping on each cupcake and bake for 20 to 25 minutes. Remove pan from the oven and cool for 5 minutes. Then remove the cupcakes and cool on a rack.

Store in an airtight container for up to 3 days, or freeze for up to 3 months.

Makes 1 dozen

glazed blueberry-lime cupcakes

see variations page 320

Low in fat with super-food blueberries — you may feel virtuous when you bake these!

for the cupcakes
1/2 cup (1 stick) margarine, softened
1 cup superfine sugar
2 eggs, lightly beaten
1 tsp. vanilla extract
1/2 cup fat-free milk
2 cups self-rising flour
1 tsp. baking powder

1 cup fresh blueberries
1 tbsp. grated lime zest

for the glaze
1/2 cup superfine sugar
2 tbsp. grated lime zest
3 tbsp. lime juice
2 tbsp. boiling water

Preheat the oven to 350°F (175°C). Place 18 paper baking cups in muffin pans. Combine the margarine and sugar with an electric mixer until soft and creamy. Add the eggs slowly and mix well. Beat in the vanilla and milk. Sift the flour and baking powder and stir into the batter until just combined. Fold in the blueberries and lime zest. Spoon the mixture into the cups. Bake for 20 minutes. Remove pans from the oven and cool for 5 minutes. Then remove the cupcakes and cool on a rack. To make the glaze, mix the sugar, lime zest, lime juice, and boiling water in a small saucepan. Bring to a gentle simmer over a medium heat, stirring to dissolve the sugar. Simmer uncovered for 5 minutes. Remove from the heat, cool slightly, and spoon over the cool cupcakes. Store in an airtight container for up to 3 days, or unglazed in the freezer for up to 3 months.

Makes 1 1/2 dozen

banana & honey cupcakes

see variations page 321

Bananas lend themselves to natural sweeteners like maple syrup and honey. Add walnuts to offset the sweetness and to give the cupcakes a little crunch.

1 3/4 cups (about 4) mashed bananas
3/4 cup packed light brown sugar
1/4 cup honey
4 tbsp. margarine, melted

2 cups self-rising flour
1 tsp. baking powder
Pinch of salt
3/4 cup (5 oz.) roughly chopped walnuts

Preheat the oven to 350°F (175°C). Place 18 paper baking cups in muffin pans.

In a large bowl, combine the bananas, sugar, honey, and margarine. Beat with an electric mixer until well blended. Slowly add the flour, baking powder, and salt, and mix well. Fold in the chopped walnuts.

Spoon the batter into the cups. Bake for 20 minutes. Remove pans from the oven and cool for 5 minutes. Remove the cupcakes and cool on a rack. Place each in a foil cup to display.

Store in an airtight container for up to 2 days, or freeze for up to 3 months.

Makes 1 1/2 dozen

pumpkin & ginger muffins

see variations page 322

These muffins are a delicious fall treat. If you can't find fresh pumpkin,
then use canned pumpkin.

2 2/3 cups all-purpose flour
1/3 cup packed light brown sugar
1 tbsp. baking powder
1/2 tsp. nutmeg
1/2 tsp. ground cloves
1 tsp. ground ginger
Pinch of salt

1 lightly beaten egg
1/2 cup puréed pumpkin, fresh or canned
3/4 cup fat-free milk
1/3 cup sunflower oil
3 tbsp. chopped candied ginger
4 tbsp. pumpkin seeds

Preheat the oven to 350°F (175°C). Grease a 12-cup muffin pan. In a medium bowl, combine
the dry ingredients with a spoon. In a large bowl, beat the egg, pumpkin, milk, and oil with
an electric mixer until well combined. Add the flour mixture to the pumpkin mixture, mixing
until nearly combined. Fold in the candied ginger, but do not overmix.

Spoon the batter into the prepared tin. Sprinkle each muffin with a few of the pumpkin seeds.

Bake for 20 minutes. Remove pan from the oven and cool for 5 minutes. Then remove the
muffins and cool on a rack.

Store in an airtight container for up to 2 days, or freeze for up to 3 months.

Makes 1 dozen

marbled mini bundt cakes

see variations page 323

Bake these cakes in little bundt pans for a really extravagant-looking cupcake. You can also use ordinary muffin pans.

1/2 cup (1 stick) margarine, softened
1 cup superfine sugar
2 lightly beaten eggs
1 tsp. vanilla extract
2 cups all-purpose flour
1 tbsp. baking powder

3/4 cup fat-free milk
2 tbsp. Dutch-process cocoa powder
1/2 cup (3 1/2 oz.) finely chopped semisweet
    chocolate
Cocoa powder for dusting

Preheat the oven to 350°F (175°C). Grease 6 mini bundt pans or a large 6-cup muffin pan. In a large bowl, beat the margarine and sugar with an electric mixer until thick and pale. Slowly add the eggs and vanilla, beating well. Mix the flour and baking powder in a medium bowl. Add to the margarine mixture in thirds, alternating with the milk.

Divide the batter into two bowls. Fold the cocoa powder and chocolate into one of the bowls. Spoon a little plain batter into the bottom of the each bundt pan, then spoon some chocolate batter on top. Continue until each pan is three-quarters full and there are 4 layers. Swirl the mixture in each cup using the point of a knife. Bake for 35 minutes. Remove pans from the oven and cool for 10 minutes. Then remove the bundt cakes and cool on a rack. Serve dusted with cocoa powder. Store in an airtight container for up to 2 days.

Makes 1/2 dozen

low-fat carrot & nut cupcakes

see variations page 324

The low-fat version of the classic American cake. If you can't get fat-free cream cheese for the frosting, use fat-free plain yogurt.

for the cupcakes
2 cups self-rising flour
1 tsp. baking powder
1/2 tsp. nutmeg
1 tsp. ground ginger
3/4 cup packed brown sugar
1/2 cup shredded carrots
1/2 cup (3 1/2 oz.) roughly chopped walnuts
3/4 cup (1 or 2) mashed bananas

2 lightly beaten eggs
2/3 cup vegetable oil

for the frosting
1 cup fat-free cream cheese, softened
1 cup confectioners' sugar, sifted
1 tsp. vanilla extract
4 tbsp. chopped walnuts
12 walnut halves

Preheat the oven to 350°F (175°C). Place 12 paper baking cups in a muffin pan. In a large bowl, combine all the cupcake ingredients. Beat on a low speed with an electric mixer until all the ingredients are combined. Spoon the mixture into the cups. Bake for 20 minutes. Remove pan from the oven and cool for 5 minutes. Remove the cupcakes and cool on a rack. To make the frosting, combine the cream cheese with the confectioners' sugar and vanilla with an electric mixer. Beat until smooth and creamy. Fold in the walnuts. Smear onto the cooled cupcakes and garnish with the walnut halves. Store unfrosted in an airtight container for up to 3 days, or freeze for up to 3 months.

Makes 1 dozen

citrus yogurt muffins

see variations page 325

The acidity of the yogurt, balanced with the subtle sweetness of the citrus oils, makes these muffins utterly mouth-watering.

2 cups all-purpose flour
3/4 cup superfine sugar
1 tbsp. grated lemon zest
1 tbsp. grated orange zest
1 tbsp. grated lime zest

1 tbsp. baking powder
Pinch of salt
1 cup fat-free plain yogurt
1/2 cup sunflower oil
1 lightly beaten egg

Preheat the oven to 400°F (200°C). Grease a 12-cup muffin pan.

In a medium bowl, combine the flour, sugar, lemon zest, orange zest, lime zest, baking powder, and salt. In a large bowl, beat the yogurt, oil, and egg until well blended. Add the flour mixture, stirring until just combined. Do not overmix.

Spoon the batter into the prepared pan. Bake for 20 minutes. Remove pan from the oven and cool for 5 minutes. Then remove the muffins and serve warm.

Store in an airtight container for up to 3 days, or freeze for up to 3 months.

Makes 1 dozen

variations

ricotta cheesecake cupcakes

see base recipe page 293

banana & raisin ricotta cupcakes
Prepare the basic recipe but use only 3 cups ricotta cheese. Add 3/4 cup (about 2 medium) mashed bananas to the ricotta cheese after adding the eggs and confectioners' sugar. Add 1/2 cup (3 1/2 oz.) raisins along with the walnuts.

blueberry ricotta cupcakes
Prepare the basic cheesecake mixture, folding in 1 cup fresh blueberries just before adding the walnuts.

raspberry & lime ricotta cupcakes
Prepare the basic cheesecake mixture, folding in 1 cup fresh raspberries and 1 tablespoon freshly grated lime zest just before adding the walnuts.

raspberry & cottage cheese muffins

see base recipe page 295

blueberry & cottage cheese muffins
Prepare the basic muffin recipe, substituting 2 cups fresh blueberries
for the raspberries.

cherry & cottage cheese muffins
Prepare the basic muffin recipe, substituting 2 cups fresh cherries
for the raspberries.

apricot & cottage cheese muffins
Prepare the basic muffin recipe, substituting 2 cups sliced fresh
apricots for the raspberries.

variations

low-fat chocolate chip muffins

see base recipe page 296

low-fat hazelnut-chocolate muffins
Prepare the basic muffin recipe, adding 3 tablespoons chopped roasted hazelnuts after adding the dry ingredients.

low-fat raspberry-chocolate muffins
Prepare the basic muffin recipe, adding 1/2 cup fresh raspberries to the batter after adding the dry ingredients.

low-fat zucchini & chocolate muffins
Prepare the basic muffin recipe. Add 1 teaspoon fresh-ground black pepper to the dry ingredients. Add 1/2 cup shredded fresh zucchini after mixing in the dry ingredients.

variations

low-fat vanilla cupcakes

see base recipe page 298

low-fat cupcakes with fennel & orange drizzle
Prepare the basic cupcake mixture. In the glaze, substitute 2 teaspoons
lightly crushed fennel seeds for the poppy seeds, and substitute
1 teaspoon orange extract for the vanilla extract.

low-fat cupcakes with strawberry & lime drizzle
Prepare the basic cupcake mixture. In the glaze, substitute 1 teaspoon
strawberry extract for the vanilla, and add 1 tablespoon freshly grated
lime zest to the mixture.

low-fat cupcakes with almond & cherry drizzle
Prepare the basic cupcake mixture. In the glaze, substitute 1 teaspoon
almond extract for the vanilla extract. Add 2 tablespoons chopped
candied cherries.

variations

flour-lite chocolate cupcakes

see base recipe page 299

flour-lite orange cupcakes
Prepare the basic cupcake recipe, substituting 2 teaspoons orange extract for the vanilla extract.

flour-lite chocolate-glazed cupcakes
Prepare the basic cupcake recipe. Make a glaze: Sift 1 1/2 cups confectioners' sugar and 2 tablespoons Dutch-process cocoa powder into a medium bowl. Beat 2 tablespoons softened margarine into the cocoa powder mixture, adding 1 tablespoon warm water and 1 tablespoon coffee liqueur to make a pourable consistency. Spoon over the cupcakes.

flour-lite chocolate & cinnamon cupcakes
Prepare the basic cupcake recipe, adding 2 teaspoons cinnamon to the dry ingredients.

variations

quick applesauce cupcakes

see base recipe page 301

pecan & applesauce cupcakes
Prepare the basic cupcake recipe, adding 3 tablespoons chopped pecans after adding the dry ingredients. For the topping, substitute 3 tablespoons chopped pecans for the walnuts.

raisin & applesauce cupcakes
Prepare the basic cupcake recipe, adding 4 tablespoons raisins after adding the dry ingredients.

cranberry & applesauce cupcakes
Prepare the basic cupcake recipe, adding 4 tablespoons dried cranberries after adding the dry ingredients.

variations

glazed blueberry–lime cupcakes

see base recipe page 302

glazed raspberry-lemon cupcakes
Prepare the basic cupcake recipe, substituting 1 cup fresh raspberries
for the blueberries, and 1 tablespoon grated lemon zest for the lime
zest in the glaze.

glazed blackberry-orange cupcakes
Prepare the basic cupcake recipe, substituting 1 cup fresh blackberries
for the blueberries, and 1 tablespoon grated orange zest for the lime
zest in the glaze.

glazed strawberry-lime cupcakes
Prepare the basic cupcake recipe, substituting 1 cup fresh sliced
strawberries for the blueberries.

variations

banana & honey cupcakes

see base recipe page 305

banana, hazelnut, & honey cupcakes
Prepare the basic cupcake recipe, substituting 3/4 cup (5 oz.) roughly
chopped unblanched hazelnuts for the walnuts.

banana & maple syrup cupcakes
Prepare the basic cupcake recipe, substituting 1/4 cup maple syrup
for the honey.

banana, pecan, & corn syrup cupcakes
Prepare the basic cupcake recipe, substituting 3/4 cup (5 oz.) roughly
chopped pecans for the walnuts, and 1/4 cup corn syrup for the honey.

pumpkin & ginger muffins

see base recipe page 306

marjoram, pumpkin, & feta cheese muffins
Prepare the basic muffin recipe, substituting 2 teaspoons minced fresh marjoram for the nutmeg, ginger, and cloves. Add 1/2 cup (4 oz.) crumbled feta to the batter after the flour has been added.

currant, pumpkin, & ginger muffins
Prepare the basic muffin recipe, folding in 1/2 cup (3 1/2 oz.) currants along with the candied ginger.

pumpkin, ginger, chili, & cilantro muffins
Prepare the basic muffin recipe, adding 1 tablespoon freshly minced chili and 1 tablespoon roughly chopped fresh cilantro.

marbled mini bundt cakes

see base recipe page 309

marbled mini raisin bundt cakes
Prepare the basic cupcake recipe. After dividing the batters add
3 tablespoons golden raisins to the plain batter.

marbled mini orange & walnut bundt cakes
Prepare the basic cupcake recipe. After dividing the batters add
1 teaspoon orange extract to the chocolate batter, and 3 tablespoons
chopped walnuts to the plain batter.

marbled mini pistachio bundt cakes
Prepare the basic cupcake recipe. After dividing the batters, add
3 tablespoons chopped pistachio nuts to the plain batter.

variations

low-fat carrot & nut cupcakes

see base recipe page 310

low-fat carrot & pecan cupcakes
Prepare the basic cupcake mixture, substituting 1/2 cup (3 1/2 oz.) of roughly chopped pecans for the walnuts. Substitute 4 tablespoons chopped pecans for the walnuts in the frosting, and substitute 12 pecans for the walnut halves for garnishing.

low-fat ginger-frosted carrot cupcakes
Prepare the basic cupcake mixture. In the frosting, substitute 3 tablespoons chopped candied ginger for the chopped walnuts.

low-fat carrot & orange cupcakes
Prepare the basic cupcake mixture, adding 1 teaspoon orange extract and 1 teaspoon ground cumin to the cupcakes.

citrus yogurt muffins

see base recipe page 313

poppy-seed yogurt muffins
Prepare the basic muffin recipe, folding in 3 tablespoons of poppy seeds
after adding the dry ingredients.

citrus-glazed yogurt muffins
Prepare the basic muffin recipe. To make the citrus glaze, combine
1 tablespoon each of lime, orange, and lemon zest with 5 tablespoons
water and 1/2 cup superfine sugar. Dissolve the sugar in a pan over
low heat. Simmer for 5 minutes. Spoon over the muffins.

citrus & blueberry yogurt muffins
Prepare the basic muffin recipe, folding in 1/3 cup (3 oz.) dried blueberries
after adding the dry ingredients.

cupcakes for special diets

Dairy-free berry cupcakes, gluten-free pecan cupcakes,

sugar-free muffins, and chocolate vegan cupcakes —

anyone with special dietary requirements will be well catered

for with the selection of recipes in this chapter.

ultimate flourless choc cupcakes

see variations page 346

For maximum luxury, top with chocolate heavy cream.

for the cupcakes
1 1/2 cups (10 1/2 oz.) bittersweet chocolate
    chips
1 cup (2 sticks) sweet butter
4 eggs
4 egg yolks
1/2 cup superfine sugar
2 tbsp. Dutch-process cocoa powder, sifted
2 tbsp. ground almonds
1 tsp. vanilla extract

for the frosting
2 tbsp. Dutch-process cocoa powder
4 tbsp. confectioners' sugar
1 1/2 cups heavy cream
1 tsp. vanilla extract
1/2 tsp. orange extract

Preheat the oven to 375°F (190°C). Place 12 paper baking cups in a muffin pan. Put the chocolate and butter in a double boiler, or medium bowl over a pan of simmering water, and stir until completely melted. Set aside to cool. In a large bowl, cream the eggs and sugar with an electric mixer until pale and thick. Gently fold in the melted chocolate and remaining ingredients. Spoon the batter into the cups. Bake for 20 minutes. Remove pan from the oven and cool for 5 minutes. Then remove the cupcakes and cool on a rack. To make the frosting, sift the cocoa and confectioners' sugar together into a medium bowl. Add the cream, vanilla, and orange extract. Beat until soft, but the cream should still hold its shape. Spoon over the warm cupcakes. Store unfrosted in an airtight container for up to 2 days.

Makes 1 dozen

chocolate vegan cupcakes

see variations page 347

To make this authentically vegan you must use specially labeled vegan chocolate chips.

2 1/2 cups all-purpose flour
4 tbsp. Dutch-process cocoa powder
Pinch of salt
2 cups superfine sugar
1/2 cup unsweetened applesauce

2 cups cold water
2 tsp. white vinegar
2 tsp. baking soda
1 cup (6 oz.) semisweet vegan chocolate chips
Cocoa powder for dusting

Preheat the oven to 375°F (190°C). Place 12 paper baking cups in a muffin pan. Sift the flour, cocoa, salt, and sugar into a large bowl and set aside.

In a separate large bowl, combine the applesauce, water, vinegar, and baking soda. Add the flour mixture and stir well to combine. Fold in the chocolate chips.

Spoon the mixture into the cups. Bake for about 20 minutes.

Remove pan from the oven and cool for 5 minutes. Then remove the cupcakes and cool on a rack. Serve dusted with cocoa.

Store in an airtight container for up to 3 days, or freeze for up to 3 months.

Makes 1 dozen

g.i. carrot cupcakes

see variations page 348

The cupcakes are perfect for those using the glycemic index to monitor their diet. Low glycemic foods release their sugars slowly — and are thus more beneficial for maintaining blood sugar levels.

1/2 cup light vegetable oil
1/2 cup packed brown sugar
1 lightly beaten egg
3 egg whites
1 cup shredded carrots
1 cup shredded cooking apples
1 cup (7 oz.) raisins

1/2 cup (3 1/2 oz.) chopped dates
1/2 cup (3 1/2 oz.) mixed dried berries
1/2 cup (3 1/2 oz.) chopped walnuts
1 tsp. allspice
1 tsp. baking powder
2 3/4 cups self-rising whole wheat flour

Preheat the oven to 350°F (175°C). Place 12 paper baking cups into a muffin pan. In a large bowl, combine the oil and sugar, and beat with an electric mixer until light and smooth, about 2 to 3 minutes. Beat the egg and egg whites, one at a time, and then add the carrots, apples, dried fruits, and walnuts. Sift the rest of the ingredients into a medium mixing bowl. Add them to the carrot mixture, stirring until just combined. Spoon the mixture into the cups. Bake for 20 minutes. Remove pan from the oven and cool for 5 minutes. Then remove the cupcakes and cool on a rack. Serve with a low-fat margarine spread.

Store in an airtight container for up to 3 days, or freeze for up to 3 months.

Makes 1 dozen

egg-free chocolate cupcakes

see variations page 349

These deliciously moist, egg-free cupcakes are simple to prepare. The cherry cola lends a subtle sweetness.

1 cup (2 sticks) sweet butter, softened
14 oz. can condensed milk
2 cups self-rising flour
1 cup Dutch-process cocoa powder

2 tsp. baking powder
1/2 cup (3 1/2 oz.) semisweet chocolate chips
1 tsp. vanilla extract
1 1/2 cups cherry cola

Preheat the oven to 350°F (175°C). Place 12 paper baking cups into a muffin pan.

In a medium bowl, cream the butter with an electric mixer until light, about 2 to 3 minutes. Add the condensed milk and beat until combined. Sift the flour, cocoa, and baking powder into the wet mixture. Stir in the chocolate chips, vanilla, and cola.

Spoon the batter into the cups. Bake for 20 minutes. Remove pan from the oven and cool for 5 minutes. Then remove the cupcakes and cool on a rack.

Store in an airtight container for up to 3 days, or freeze for up to 3 months.

Makes 1 dozen

soy milk muffins

see variations page 350

Soy milk is a perfect replacement for regular cow's milk. It is fortified with all the vitamins and minerals of its dairy counterpart.

1 1/4 cups whole wheat flour
1 tbsp. baking powder
1 cup (6 oz.) raisins
1 tsp. chopped fresh rosemary
1/2 cup (3 1/2 oz.) chopped blanched almonds

1/2 cup (3 1/2 oz.) chopped pecans
1 tsp. orange extract
1/2 cup olive oil
1/2 cup soy milk
1/2 cup honey

Preheat the oven to 400°F (200°C). Grease a 12-cup muffin pan. In a medium bowl, mix the flour, baking powder, raisins, rosemary, almonds, and pecans. In a large bowl, beat the orange extract, oil, soy milk, and honey until combined. Slowly fold the dried ingredients into the soy mixture until just combined.

Spoon the mixture into the prepared pan.

Bake for 20 minutes. Remove pan from the oven and cool for 5 minutes. Then remove the muffins and cool on a rack.

Store in an airtight container for up to 2 days, or freeze for up to 3 months.

Makes 1 dozen

sugar-free grain muffins

see variations page 351

These great little muffins are packed full of fiber and contain no refined sweeteners.

1 cup mixed-grain cereal	4 tbsp. honey
2 cups boiling water	Pinch of salt
1 1/2 cups all-purpose flour	1 lightly beaten egg
1 tbsp. baking powder	1/3 cup safflower oil

In a medium bowl, mix the cereal and water. Set aside for 20 minutes for the grains to swell.

Preheat the oven to 400°F (200°C). Grease a 12-cup muffin pan. In a medium bowl sift the flour and baking powder.

In a large bowl, beat the honey, salt, egg, and oil. Slowly add the flour and the cereal and mix well.

Spoon the mixture into the prepared pan. Bake in the oven for 20 minutes. Remove pan from the oven and cool for 5 minutes. Then remove the muffins and cool on a rack.

Store in an airtight container for up to 3 days, or freeze for up to 3 months.

Makes 1 dozen

dairy-free berry cupcakes

see variations page 352

These little treats are wonderful for the lactose-intolerant cupcake lover.

for the cupcakes
2 1/2 cups mixed fresh berries (blueberries,
    strawberries, cranberries, blackberries)
2 cups all-purpose flour
1/2 cup packed brown sugar
1 tbsp. baking powder

4 tbsp. vegetable oil
2 lightly beaten eggs

for the topping
1/2 cup mixed berry jam

Preheat the oven to 350°F (175°C). Place 12 paper baking cups into a muffin pan. In a food processor, purée 1 1/2 cups of the berries until smooth. In a small bowl, lightly crush the reserved berries with a fork. In a medium bowl, mix the flour, sugar, and baking powder. In a large bowl, beat the oil and eggs. Add the puréed berries and mix well. Stir in the flour mixture until combined. Fold in the crushed berries.

Spoon the batter into the cups. Top each cupcake with a teaspoon of jam. Bake for 20 minutes. Remove pan from the oven and cool for 5 minutes. Then remove the cupcakes and cool on a rack.

Store in an airtight container for up to 3 days, or freeze for up to 3 months.

Makes 1 dozen

gluten-free macadamia nut & raisin muffins

see variations page 353

Serve these to friends or kids as a treat and they will never know how healthy they are!

1 cup soya bran
1 cup (5 oz.) finely ground, roasted
    macadamia nuts
3/4 cup packed brown sugar
1 tbsp. baking powder
2 lightly beaten eggs

4 tbsp. vegetable oil
4 tbsp. butter, melted and cooled
3/4 cup milk
1/2 cup (3 1/2 oz.) raisins
4 tbsp. roughly chopped macadamia nuts

Preheat the oven to 375°F (190°C). Grease a 12-cup muffin pan.

In a medium bowl, mix the bran, nuts, sugar, and baking powder. In a large bowl, beat the eggs, oil, butter, and milk. Add the flour, mixing until nearly combined. Fold in the raisins and macadamia nuts.

Spoon the mixture into the prepared pan. Bake for about 20 minutes. Remove pan from the oven and cool for 5 minutes. Then remove the muffins and cool on a rack.

Store in an airtight container for up to 3 days, or freeze for up to 3 months.

Makes 1 dozen

gluten-free pecan cupcakes

see variations page 354

Gluten-free flour has a variety of uses. Look for it in specialty food or health stores. Add a little more liquid than you would when using normal flour, since it will be absorbed.

2 3/4 cups gluten-free all-purpose flour
3/4 cup superfine sugar
1 1/2 tbsp. baking powder
Pinch of salt
2 lightly beaten eggs

4 tbsp. sweet butter, melted
1 1/4 cups milk
1 tsp. vanilla extract
1 cup (5 oz.) roughly chopped pecans
1/2 cup (3 1/2 oz.) chopped dates

Preheat the oven to 400°F (200°C). Grease a 12-cup muffin pan.

In a medium bowl, mix the flour, sugar, baking powder, and salt. In a large bowl, beat the eggs, butter, milk, and vanilla. Add the dry ingredients and stir until nearly combined. Fold in the pecans and dates.

Spoon the mixture into the prepared pan. Bake for 20 minutes. Remove pan from the oven and cool for 5 minutes. Then remove the muffins and cool on a rack.

Store in an airtight container for up to 3 days, or freeze for up to 3 months.

Makes 1 dozen

avocado & lemon muffins

see variations page 355

Avocados contain a host of essential oils, vitamins, and minerals — all beneficial for the body's nervous system.

2 medium haas avocados, peeled
   and roughly chopped
1 tsp. lemon juice
2 1/2 cups all-purpose flour
Pinch of salt
1 tbsp. baking powder

2 lightly beaten eggs
1 cup milk
4 tbsp. extra virgin olive oil
4 tbsp. sweet butter, melted
1 1/2 tbsp. lemon zest
1 tsp. freshly ground black pepper

Preheat the oven to 400°F (200°C). Grease a 12-cup muffin pan.

Place the avocado in a bowl with the lemon juice. Crush lightly with a fork. In a medium bowl, mix the flour, salt, and baking powder. Beat the remaining ingredients in a large bowl. Add the flour mixture, stirring until nearly combined. Fold in the avocado. Do not overmix.

Spoon the mixture into the prepared pan. Bake for 20 minutes. Remove pan from the oven and cool for 5 minutes. Then remove the muffins and cool on a rack.

Store in an airtight container for up to 2 days or freeze for up to 3 months.

Makes 1 dozen

variations

ultimate flourless choc cupcakes

see base recipe page 327

ultimate flourless peppermint cream cupcakes
Prepare the basic cupcake recipe. Substitute 1 teaspoon peppermint extract
for the vanilla and orange extract.

ultimate flourless vanilla ice cream cupcakes
Prepare the basic cupcake recipe. Make an ice cream topping: Mix 2 cups
ready-made pudding and 1 1/4 cups heavy cream in a large bowl, and
beat well. Add 1 teaspoon vanilla extract. Pour into an ice cream maker
and churn until frozen. Put 1 scoop on top of each cupcake.

ultimate flourless strawberry cream cupcakes
Prepare the basic cupcake recipe. In the frosting, substitute 1 teaspoon
strawberry extract for the vanilla extract. Fold 1/2 cup finely chopped
fresh strawberries after beating the cream.

variations

chocolate vegan cupcakes

see base recipe page 328

chocolate & orange vegan cupcakes

Prepare the basic cupcake recipe, adding 1 1/2 tablespoons grated orange zest to the mixture along with the chocolate chips.

chocolate & hazelnut vegan cupcakes

Prepare the basic cupcake recipe, adding 1/2 cup (3 1/2 oz.) chopped roasted hazelnuts along with the chocolate chips.

chocolate & coffee vegan cupcakes

Prepare the basic cupcake recipe, adding 1/4 cup hot coffee to the applesauce mixture.

variations

g.i. carrot cupcakes

see base recipe page 331

g.i. pecan cupcakes
Prepare the basic cupcake mixture, substituting 1/2 cup (3 1/2 oz.) chopped pecans for the walnuts.

g.i. banana cupcakes
Prepare the basic cupcake mixture, adding 1/2 cup mashed bananas along with the carrots and fruits. Substitute 1/2 teaspoon nutmeg for the allspice.

g.i. currant cupcakes
Prepare the basic cupcake mixture, substituting 1 cup (7 oz.) currants for the raisins.

variations

egg-free chocolate cupcakes

see base recipe page 332

egg-free white chocolate cupcakes
Prepare the basic cupcake recipe, substituting 1/2 cup (3 1/2 oz.) white chocolate chips for the semisweet chocolate chips.

egg-free chocolate pecan cupcakes
Prepare the basic cupcake recipe, adding 1/2 cup (3 1/2 oz.) chopped pecans along with the chocolate chips.

egg-free chocolate macadamia cupcakes
Prepare the basic cupcake recipe, adding 1/2 cup (3 1/2 oz.) chopped macadamia nuts along with the chocolate chips.

variations

soy milk muffins

see base recipe page 335

soy milk & cranberry muffins
Prepare the basic muffin recipe, substituting 1 cup (7 oz.) dried cranberries for the raisins.

soy milk & apricot muffins
Prepare the basic muffin recipe, substituting 1 cup (7 oz.) chopped dried apricots for the raisins.

soy milk & blueberry muffins
Prepare the basic muffin recipe, substituting 1 cup (7 oz.) dried blueberries for the raisins.

sugar-free grain muffins

see base recipe page 336

sugar-free prune muffins
Prepare the basic muffin recipe, adding 4 tablespoons chopped dried prunes to the muffin batter.

sugar-free banana muffins
Prepare the basic muffin recipe, adding 1/2 cup mashed bananas to the muffin batter.

sugar-free pecan muffins
Prepare the basic muffin recipe, adding 1/2 cup (3 1/2 oz.) chopped pecans to the muffin batter.

variations

dairy-free berry cupcakes

see base recipe page 339

dairy-free apple & berry cupcakes
Prepare the basic muffin recipe, substituting 1 1/2 cups unsweetened applesauce for 1 1/2 cups of the mixed berries.

dairy-free nectarine & berry cupcakes
Prepare the basic muffin recipe, substituting 1 1/2 cups puréed canned nectarines for 1 1/2 cups of the mixed berries.

dairy-free peach & berry cupcakes
Prepare the basic muffin recipe, substituting 1 1/2 cups puréed canned peaches for 1 1/2 cups of the mixed berries.

gluten-free macadamia nut & raisin muffins

see base recipe page 340

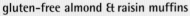

gluten-free almond & raisin muffins
Prepare the basic muffin recipe, substituting 1 cup (5 oz.) ground almonds for the ground macadamia nuts. Replace the 4 tablespoons chopped macadamia nuts with 4 tablespoons chopped blanched almonds.

gluten-free macademia nut & cranberry muffins
Prepare the basic muffin recipe, substituting 1/2 cup (3 1/2 oz.) dried cranberries for the golden raisins.

gluten-free macademia nut & cherry muffins
Prepare the basic muffin recipe, substituting 1/2 cup (3 1/2 oz.) dried cherries for the golden raisins.

variations

gluten-free pecan cupcakes

see base recipe page 343

gluten-free mixed peel cupcakes
Prepare the basic cupcake recipe, substituting 1/2 cup (3 1/2 oz.) chopped candied mixed peel for the dates.

gluten-free apricot cupcakes
Prepare the basic cupcake recipe, substituting 1/2 cup (3 1/2 oz.) chopped dried apricots for the dates.

gluten-free molasses cupcakes
Prepare the basic cupcake recipe, omitting the sugar and adding 4 tablespoons molasses and 4 tablespoons of honey to the milk mixture.

avocado & lemon muffins

see base recipe page 344

chili, avocado, & lemon muffins
Prepare the basic muffin recipe, adding 1 tablespoon seeded and finely chopped chili to the egg mixture.

avocado & orange muffins
Prepare the basic muffin recipe, substituting 1 tablespoon grated orange zest for the lemon zest.

avocado & tomato muffins
Prepare the basic muffin recipe, adding 3 tablespoons chopped sun-dried tomatoes to the batter after the flour has been added.

index